In Defense of
Adversity

STEVE GAVATORTA

Published by Richter Publishing LLC www.richterpublishing.com

Editors: Margarita Martinez, Savannah Grooms, Monica San Nicolas, and Natalie Meyer

Cover Design: Jessie Alarcon

ISBN-10:1-945812-20-6
ISBN-13:978-1-945812-20-0

DISCLAIMER

This book is designed to provide information on adversity only. This information is provided and sold with the knowledge that the publisher and author do not offer any legal or medical advice. In the case of a need for any such expertise, consult with the appropriate professional. This book does not contain all information available on the subject. This book has not been created to be specific to any individual's or organization's situation or needs. Every effort has been made to make this book as accurate as possible. However, there may be typographical and/ or content errors. Therefore, this book should serve only as a general guide and not as the ultimate source of subject information. This book contains information that might be dated and is intended only to educate and entertain. The author and publisher shall have no liability or responsibility to any person or entity regarding any loss or damage incurred, or alleged to have been incurred, directly or indirectly, by the information contained in this book. You hereby agree to be bound by this disclaimer or you may return this book within the guarantee time period for a full refund. In the interest of full disclosure, this book contains affiliate links that might pay the author or publisher a commission upon any purchase from the company. While the author and publisher take no responsibility for the business practices of these companies and/ or the performance of any product or service, the author or publisher has used the product or service and makes a recommendation in good faith based on that experience. All characters appearing in this work have given permission to be quoted and printed within this book. Any resemblance to other real persons, living or dead, is purely coincidental. This information is the sole opinion of the author and not the publisher.

DEDICATION

First, I dedicate this book to my high school English teacher, Lorraine Dellaria. Although I wasn't necessarily the best student, your instruction did indeed sink in. You provided me with an excellent foundation for organizing my thoughts so I could effectively write and communicate. Thank you for your instruction and patience. I'm sure as a teacher you often wonder if your instruction resonates. You may not have thought so at the time, however, I assure you it did with me.

I'd also like to dedicate the book to Mark Marshall, one of my best friends since childhood. At the writing of this book, Mark suffered a heart attack. In true fashion, he dealt with it positively and is now nearly back to good health. His grit and determination optimizes the content in this book. He is a perfect role model for someone who takes on difficulties head-on, in a level-headed way, and wins ... or at least learns lessons that prepare him to succeed in the future. God Bless, Mark.

Next, to all those immigrant families from Burgettstown and the village of Langeloth, who came to America with very little and not only survived, but thrived, making not only our town, but the United States of America the greatest, most prosperous country on the planet.

Lastly, to all of those who faced unbelievable difficulties and adversity during Hurricanes Harvey and Irma. Your grit, determination, love, and compassion was an inspiration to all.

ACKNOWLEDGEMENTS

I want to acknowledge all the people in my life who have influenced and motivated me to live a life of constant improvement. People who not only motivated me, but also who were patient and communicated with me in ways I could understand, which resonated with me, through which I could learn and grow. They pushed me and enabled me to the best person I could become.

First and foremost, I would like to acknowledge my friend and mentor Santo Laquatra, whose guidance and wisdom I've been receiving for nearly 33 years. My friend is never too busy or too tired to take the time to help not only me, but others as well. Truly selfless, he is a role model that I aspire to emulate.

My first personal coach, friend, mentor, and oftentimes business partner, Meryl Moritz, whose sage advice provided me with the courage and guidance to get my business off the ground.

To my participants who helped me with content and PR recommendations for the book: Barry Alvarez, Dr. Pete Stracci, Petro and Despina Maropis, Toni Locy, Tracey Petricca, Adoni Maropis, Chris Maropis, and Eric Parker

To the participants in my adversity survey and multiple interviews: Justin Moore, Peter Vaas, Karina Thomson, Sarah Peeples, Rob Newman, Jay Hayes, Robert Fraser, Brian Petrucci, Dave Pruitt, Matt Arroyo, Billy Quarantillo, Matt Frevola, Jennifer Shirkani, Abby Goodwin Roni Sloman, Jeff Filkovski, Ken O'Keefe, Barrie Pressly, Keith Tandy, Keeno Griffin, Dave Sedmak, Pamela Sedmak, Margie Bahm, Todd Fox, Bill Bonnstetter, Joe Rossi, Kevin Palermo, Brian Hill, Adam Gross, Michael Barrette, Ed Pinkham, Mark Liebel, Candace Andersson, Holly Blake, Mark Hunter, Sarah Sponaugle, Luis Echeverry Robert Tudi, Kim Milite, Brian Tucker, Karen Lindsey, Brady Quinn, Pete Comis, Topher Cramm, Chris Maropis, Chad Hymas, John Mahoney, and Adoni Maropis.

Tara Richter, my publisher, for providing the structure and roadmap to write this book and get it published.

And last but not least, to my parents, Steve and Donna Gavatorta, and my close friends, contributors Mark Marshall, Greg Capretto, Mandy Minor, Dave Fisher, Lisa Sideris, and Lee McCargar for their support and honest opinions.

CONTENTS

FROM COAL TO DIAMONDS

The gem cannot be perfected without friction, nor can man be perfected without trials.
~
-Chinese Proverb-

Barry Alvarez—The Wisconsin Badgers' Football Coach

It was a beautiful, warm day. The sun was shining, not a cloud in the sky. However, this was not just another normal day in Pasadena, California. History had been made. The Wisconsin band was playing "On, Wisconsin!" Fans were cheering; players shouted with joy. This was the Wisconsin Badgers' first Rose Bowl game—and they'd won, defeating hometown favorite UCLA, 21-16.

Head football coach Barry Alvarez was proud. He was the man who had turned a perennial loser into a winner in just a few short years, bringing the team here, to the "Granddaddy of Them All," the Rose Bowl.

As Barry Alvarez left the field, thoughts and emotions swirled in his head such as how far they'd come as a team, but most importantly, how far he'd come in his life. From very humble beginnings as a kid from a small coal-mining town in western Pennsylvania, just one generation removed from his Spanish ancestry, to heading off a football field that carried with it so much pride and tradition, it had been one hell of a journey. And there was more to come.

Adoni Maropis—The Hollywood Actor

On his first drive to the Hollywood set of the hit television show *24*, Adoni Maropis was heading to one of the biggest opportunities of his acting career. Slated to appear in several episodes, this was not just an opportunity for him to perform on a primetime show, but also to work with one of Hollywood's biggest stars, Kiefer Sutherland—the show's lead character, Jack Bauer. Adoni had invested hours of preparation.

His role was that of a terrorist opposing Jack Bauer. To embody this character, he needed to draw on strong emotional experiences. Knowing that his character's brother's murder was his motivation, he thought back to growing up with his two brothers, Sam and Chris, and drew from those close relationships. The process of getting into the character of a terrorist helped him prepare for the scene, but also drained him emotionally. No matter, he thought. This was the opportunity of a lifetime.

The excitement and anticipation rose as he approached the set, and Adoni couldn't help but think about his life's journey—from first-generation Greek kid from a small town in western Pennsylvania, struggling with the never-ending demands of living with Type 1 diabetes, to overcoming the difficulties of maneuvering through Hollywood, with all of its competition and rejection. Now, he was on the precipice of attaining his dream career as a professional actor. It had been a long, tough road from the streets of that small town to Hollywood, but one that was well worth the effort—and it boded well for what was to come.

Dr. Pete Stracci—The Respected Cardiologist

As I spoke with Dr. Pete Stracci, I could feel his unique blend of confidence and humility—an all-too rare combination these days. Dr. Stracci is a highly respected and successful cardiologist in the Pittsburgh area, working at one of the most prestigious cardiology institutions in the U.S., Allegheny General Hospital—an impressive achievement for an impressive individual.

Dr. Stracci gives much-deserved credit for his success to his Italian-born parents, Domenic and Fortunata. Dr. Stracci is a shining example of grit, perseverance, and hard work—all character strengths learned from his parents, strengths that also included a strong emphasis on education, greatly driven by his mother.

Dr. Stracci's long journey started in a small Italian village and led him to America at age nine, where he began fourth grade with no English proficiency. The journey further included a brief period of playing professional football for the Cleveland Browns before he became an expert physician.

Reflecting on how far he'd come, Dr. Stracci couldn't help but think about what an adventure it had been. As he put it, he's a graduate of "The School of Hard Knocks." But for him, there is no regret. It was that school that made him who he is today—a worthy education, indeed.

The Common Denominator #1: Poor Immigrants Coming for Opportunity

These are just three examples of ordinary people who went on to become extraordinary in their fields of endeavor. They are part of a lineage of highly successful immigrant families who faced great odds, overcame significant adversity, and prospered in the rough coal mine town of Burgettstown, PA, most often producing successful offspring as well. These three people and their stories were not the exception; they were the norm. What do these three highly successful people, and others in their community, have in common?

These people came from a town of many immigrant families—Polish, Irish, Italian, Syrian, Greek, Armenian, German, Spanish, African—nearly every nationality around the globe. They came to America with little to nothing, not speaking each other's languages, let alone English, not having the minimal necessities like indoor plumbing. In addition, they had no welfare, no safety net, and little-to-no government assistance. These people, from a tough, unforgiving environment, turned into truly exceptional people, diamonds in their own right.

Common Denominator #2: Adversity as the Pressure that Transformed Them into Diamonds

The high success rate of these families was, in my opinion, due to their ability to face and overcome adversity. They were strong-willed and persistent, seeking the American dream, and no obstacle, big or small, could stop them. They knew that in America, they had options.

I marvel at how many successful individuals came from Burgettstown, my hometown. It produced athletes, actors, authors, inventors, lawyers, physicians, educators, politicians, scientists, businessmen and women—people from essentially every profession. Ordinary people who came from nothing and became successful.

Not only did they face many struggles upon their arrival to America, but the journeys in and of themselves were filled with difficulty. After coming to America, Barry Alvarez's father had to return to Spain and was jailed for political reasons because he opposed the Spanish dictator Francisco Franco. After a brief stay, he eventually made it back to America.

When Speros Maropis, grandfather of Adoni, first came to America, he was jailed, as he didn't have a sponsor. He was shipped back to Greece, eventually found a sponsor, and made it back to America.

Pete Stracci's father came and worked in America for five years before he saved enough money to bring his wife and three children over to once again be a family.

Tough times and individuals, indeed—but these situations made them, rather than broke them.

I believe these individuals' experiences and initial difficulties paved the way for dealing with future trials and tribulations with hard work, grit, and determination.

SAGE INSIGHTS

My paternal great grandfather fled his country with little more than a suitcase, a bride, and a baby, and started a business based on his passions. It is still in place today, I believe, because of the passion that it supports and the community that surrounds it.

-*Brian Petrucci, Corporate Training & Development Manager at Acme Construction Supply (born and raised in Burgettstown, PA)*

A Stark Contrast from Today

I overlay that tough area and timeframe with the way people today cope (or don't cope) with adversity, and conflict.

My intent is not to paint everyone with a broad brush; every day, people still face and overcome problems, learning and growing from them. However, there appear to be more excuses for failure and too many unrealistic safeguards to avoid facing obstacles. This avoidance, in my opinion, is counterproductive, as it doesn't prepare people for the real world.

Why, with so much more opportunity and assistance available, do so many people today fail, quit, and complain in the face of obstacles? Why are so many people afraid to face and deal with difficulties? Afraid of change? Afraid of risk? Why do they do everything to avoid conflict or discomfort or feeling out of their element?

Is there a way to educate people that adversity should not be feared or avoided, but rather leveraged to learn, grow, and become stronger—much like so many of those above-mentioned individuals and families?

Those questions, as well as many others, will be reviewed and discussed in this book.

In Defense of Adversity—An Overview

In our high tech, fast-paced, rapidly changing world, adversity is hitting us at speeds significantly faster than ever—and at a younger age—leaving us little time to respond and arming us with far too few tools for controlling our responses in a productive manner. When an individual lacks the tools to handle challenges, it's easy for a person to become frustrated, averse to risk, and afraid.

In Defense of Adversity alleviates this problem, bridging the gap between what we're naturally inclined to do and what works best in the modern environment. By educating readers that adversity, failure, change, and conflict can paradoxically be catalysts for positive things and help us evolve into who we were born to be, this book prepares the reader to succeed in today's chaotic environment, much like those individuals from my hometown.

Premise and Overarching Theme

Adversity is in the eye of the beholder; how a person perceives challenges determines life's journey. The purpose of this book is to act as a roadmap and supply a foundation to help people thrive in adversity and not just survive it. Addressing adversity purposefully in this way requires a plan; how to formulate that plan using an integrated process and expert insights is the theme of this book. This book's foundational pillars are based on four parts: powerful expert insights and stories from over 60 highly successful individuals across multiple professions; brain functionality; a valid behavioral assessment; and lastly, my vast 34-year professional experience working in corporate America as a consultant and business owner.

Foundational Pillar #1: Expert Insights (called Sage Insights)

As part of connecting the dots for you, I interviewed and surveyed over 60 highly successful individuals across multiple professions. The individuals who supplied their insights surrounding the topic of adversity include:

- Speakers, consultants, coaches, and trainers (personal and business-oriented)
- Athletes and sports coaches
  - Football - NFL, collegiate, and high school level
  - Wrestling - collegiate level
  - Mixed Martial Arts (MMA) - professional, amateur
  - Basketball - specialty
- Arts and Entertainment
- Education
- Entrepreneur/Business/Executive/Professional/Military

These individuals' insights will be peppered throughout the book and further shared in the closing chapter.

Foundational Pillar #2: Brain Functionality

Human instinct is to react emotionally to adversity as our primitive

ancestors did, using the limbic part of the brain, an approach that worked well for the caveman. Since then, the human brain has developed a cortex that lets us learn and grow from adversity, instead of just reacting. It gives us the ability to use the lessons of experience in thinking and acting purposefully when faced with adversity anew. In this way, people develop and thrive. We will learn about brain functionality in this book, and how you can leverage this knowledge when facing adversity.

Foundational Pillar #3: Behavioral Assessment

A validated behavioral assessment is included in this book which will show people how to create a mental process for facing adversity, whether it's a difficult boss, colleague, friend, traffic accident, unexpected change, a demanding client, or a public relations fiasco. *In Defense of Adversity* will increase your ability to successfully handle adversity by learning to proactively address difficulties with a more logical, reasoned, rational approach, versus an uncontrolled emotional one.

Foundational Pillar #4: My Professional Experiences

Lastly, much of the content from this book is based on my 34 years working in corporate America. For over 14 years I have owned Steve Gavatorta Group, a consulting, training, and coaching company. Prior to that I spent 20 years working in a variety of roles in various Fortune 500 companies.

During my career I've had the opportunity to experience a wide variety of roles in sales, management, leadership, training, marketing, etc. In my current role, I have the opportunity to work with a variety of clients across multiple industries. Due to my background, I bring valuable experience and knowledge to all my customer interactions, as well as leading, coaching, and training thousands of individuals. Much of what is shared in this book is based on my personal experiences and deeply supports the approach in the book. I've *walked the walk,* so to speak.

Within these pages, readers will find insights from people who overcame great odds to become presidents, athletes, authors, entrepreneurs, leaders, etc. This book is not only meant to provide a strong foundation for you in your daily battles with adversity, but also to inspire and motivate you in your travels on this journey called life.

Real-World Application

The key to getting the most out of this book is to apply both the learnings and tools to your life. There are many real-world examples that will serve as guideposts for you. In addition, you have the opportunity to take a valid, scientifically-backed assessment for *free*. This assessment will enable you to best understand your behavior style and your response to adverse situations. You will then learn how to use this knowledge to better identify and overcome challenges. This assessment can personalize the benefits from this book and the application of learnings to your life.

Long-Term Benefits

The lessons, tools, and examples you will read and learn can be viewed many times over. Inspirational stories and insights are always helpful. But when connected to personalized insights, this brings true value and retention of learnings. So, feel free to visit this book as often as you need and use the skills as you advance in your life personally and professionally.

The book is a living document, as is your development as a human being. At the end of each chapter, there will be a **Reader Call to Action** section. This lists specific steps and action plans you can take to help you achieve success, providing a daily roadmap to help you during your journey through life.

Book Flow

As you progress in this book, the focus will be on creating a foundation to enable you to "grind" better. This is a term you'll see at various points in the book. Basically, "grind" means the ability to remain persistent and persevering in the face of obstacles. This book is your key to creating a strong foundation for effectively leveraging adversity to your advantage.

As human beings, we're often our own worst enemies. I know I've created unnecessary problems for myself many times. Despite building a foundation for myself, I still make mistakes. It still can be a battle. The key, however, is this—I have a pathway, a foundation to get myself back on track during those times where I may feel lost. This book aims to do the same for you. This book is broken into three parts and follows a logical sequence of steps:

- **Part I: Accept and Acknowledge Adversity** (Chapters 1-2)— Possibly the biggest step you can take in learning to overcome obstacles is to realize and accept that adversity is a part of life and acknowledge that it is meant for us to grow. You need to view adversity as productively and positively as possible. Stop avoiding problems and instead, look at them opportunities. Fall back on learnings and insights from this book to solve them ... OR recognize that, regardless of the outcome, there is a learning here that can help you in future situations. That outlook and paradigm shift is huge in and of itself.

- **Part II: Journey of Self-Discovery**— (Chapters 3-10)

    - **Understanding Brain Functionality** (Chapter 3)— Understanding how the brain functions during difficulties is key to overcoming adversity. By understanding brain functionality, you can learn the importance of handling adversity in a productive manner.

    - **Build Self-Knowledge & Self-Awareness** (Chapters 4-10)—The second most important thing you can do is raise your own self-knowledge, and awareness about yourself. The more you're knowledgeable and aware of yourself, the more you can recognize what puts you in a non-productive emotional state. By becoming aware of the root cause, you can better take action.

- **Part III: Build & Maintain a Strong Foundation** (Chapters 11-14)—The good news regarding strengthening your foundation and resolve amid problems is that you can hone those skills every day. Each day offers opportunities to keep building the foundation and a reservoir of experiences, creating more options for you to overcome obstacles. The more options you have in the arsenal, the more likely you will be able to succeed.

Helpful Guides

This book will also provide helpful guides you can use to better connect the dots of learnings gleaned.

- **Reader Call to Action**—At the end of each chapter there will be Reader Call to Action questions for you to answer. These questions will facilitate your skills to effectively deal with and overcome adversity. You can write your responses in this book, or download the **In Defense of Adversity Workbook** (see instructions in the Developmental Tools section below).

- **Sage Insights**—The insights from the over 60 people I interviewed and surveyed will be peppered throughout this book. Their insights are meant to motivate, inspire, and provide wisdom to help you.

- **Book Terminology**—This book will have various words and phrases that are key to understand. Their uses may differ somewhat from the definitions you are most familiar with.

- **Developmental Tools**—During the course of this book, there will be several opportunities to access developmental tools. These tools are located at the Steve Gavatorta Group website: www.gavatorta.com click on the *In Defense of Adversity* book icon and look for the IDOA Resources section.

  So, let's begin taking the necessary steps to strengthen your resolve to learn from, face, and overcome adversity, transitioning from coal to diamonds in the process.

SAGE INSIGHTS

The value of hard work, sacrifice, and commitment is only realized through a certain degree of personal pain. This pain is the heat that forges steel or pressure that creates diamonds. It changes people. They become special because they have endured and learned. The first thing you learn is that you have separated yourself from most of society and that builds pride and confidence that nothing can stop you.

- Ken O'Keefe, Quarterback Coach, Iowa Hawkeyes

DEVELOPMENTAL TOOLS

If you prefer to capture your **Reader Call to Action** notes in the **In Defense of Adversity Workbook** rather that writing in this book, you can visit www.gavatorta.com. Then click on *In Defense of Adversity* book cover icon, and download it from the **IDOA Resources** section.

READER CALL TO ACTION

1.   List 3-5 Takeaways/Learnings from the Introduction.

2.   List 3-5 goals you want to achieve in reading this book.

PART I
ACCEPT & ACKNOWLEDGE

CHAPTER 1

AD ASTRA PER ASPERA…THROUGH HARDSHIP TO THE STARS

Life is either a daring adventure, or nothing.

~

-Helen Keller-

Burgettstown and the Little Village of Langeloth

The origin of the three men in my opening story is a small town in western Pennsylvania called Burgettstown. The small village within that town, where these three grew up, is called Langeloth. My dad was from there, too. Langeloth was the home of the American Zinc & Chemical Company, many coalmines, and later, a molybdenum plant. The opportunities for steady work, stability, and upward mobility naturally resulted in the influx of immigrants from all over the world.

There were many towns in western Pennsylvania that were similar, producing highly successful people from humble and diverse origins. The truth, I'm sure, can be similarly said about many small towns in America, but there definitely seemed something special about this area.

Something in the Water

Even if you go outside Burgettstown to neighboring towns, you find similar humble, successful immigrant families. Many say there's "something in the water" in this area that develops outstanding football coaches—men of hard work ethic, success, and leadership, who become influencers of others. If you scan a 30-mile radius of Burgettstown, you'll find the hometown origins of the following coaches: college and pro coaching legend Lou Holtz; Bill Cowher, former Steelers coach; Marvin Lewis, head coach of the Cincinnati Bengals; and Lewis' current and previous assistant coaches, Jonathon Hayes and Jay Hayes. Also from the same area were former NFL coach Marty Schottenheimer; Iowa head coach Kirk Ferentz; Gary Tranquill, former head coach at Navy; Robert Fraser, assistant coach for the Ohio State Buckeyes; and of course, Burgettstown native Barry Alvarez. Something in the water, indeed.

Iron Sharpens Iron

The high success rate of the people in this area is undeniable. Their experiences overcoming difficulties were key to that success. They accepted challenges not only as part of life, but as essential in their development as human beings. That was what was in the water in this area. I think Barry Alvarez summed it up best when he told me that people from that area "knew how to grind."

BOOK TERMINOLOGY
Grind—Grinding, in Barry Alvarez terms, simply means paying the price, with the ability to remain persistent and persevere in the face of obstacles … and learning lessons as you go through life. A key part of this book is teaching you "how to grind" in face of adversity.

Let's accept that adversity is the norm, and that our trials and tribulations will always be with us. The key is to leverage our difficulties to make us stronger and wiser each day. This insight is even more important and relevant today. So, let's all learn how to grind, which is the purpose of this book.

Our Fast-Paced, Ever-Changing World

Modern technologies drive new changes every day in this century. Continual changes in job security via downsizing, mergers, acquisitions, instability, and change are becoming the norm, and with that come both opportunities and difficulties that are hitting us faster than ever.

With that, the need to learn to overcome these challenges takes on a new importance. If we cannot adapt to this ever-changing, fast-paced environment in a productive, proactive manner, it will eat us up.

The question becomes... how are we doing as a society? Are we prepared? Are we setting the stage for success and taking advantage of the opportunities in adversity? Are we as resilient and successful as our predecessors? Yes, obviously many people are still achieving great things every day. Facing and overcoming challenges remains in great fashion all the time. Unfortunately, there seems to be a negative trend starting to rear its ugly head.

21st Century Dynamics—The Avoidance Issue

It seems like we live in a world now where people are doing everything they can to avoid facing any trial or tribulation. Many people escape their problems with drugs, both legal and illegal. This doesn't bode well, and the results don't pan out. We are more worried about protecting our self-esteem than attaining the wisdom, strength, and knowledge we can gain from our difficulties. We aren't preparing ourselves to be successful by learning lessons that can carry long-term benefits. Rather, we are seeking the comfort of short-lived, unrealistic security. This has the potential to either eliminate, or at least stunt, our growth as individuals.

Now, I'm not saying we should seek to cause unnecessary difficulties in our lives. In addition, sometimes very serious adverse situations strike that are totally out of our control, such as illnesses and accidents. However, we should not hide, ignore them, or hope that such problems simply will go away. If we are not tested, we don't learn or develop as human beings. Just think of what you might not accomplish—achieving goals, financial security, unsurpassed success, meaningful and fulfilling relationships—if you choose to hide instead of facing the issue and learning from it.

SAGE INSIGHTS

We have a train that runs past our practice facility. You cannot see it, but you can hear it, and at times it blows its horn. I draw a correlation between that train and adversity with our team. Just like that train, you will not always see adversity coming, but it is coming, and how you react to it will determine how efficiently you can move forward. I am a firm believer in enthusiasm, and I believe it can get you through anything. Adversity is that demon that will pull you down if your lack of enthusiasm allows it to.

- *Jeff Filkovski, Head Football Coach at North Carolina Wesleyan*

Does Everyone Really Deserve a Trophy?

We are becoming more of an entitled society, where everyone receives a trophy, so that many refer to the youth of today as "special snowflakes." Again, the self-esteem thing. I really don't see the positive lesson to be learned by everyone receiving a trophy. That appeasement robs people of the learning that comes from both success and failure. Winning shows what challenging work, dedication, and teamwork can do. Losing allows us to examine the reasons for the loss, and better prepares us for future success. Our failures provide as many, if not more, lessons than our successes. As Pete Stracci says, *"People from our area, and especially me, were all graduates from the school of hard knocks."*

Participation Trophy Lesson from a Pittsburgh Steeler

Recently, Pittsburgh Steeler star linebacker James Harrison caught a lot of flak on social media for making his two boys, aged five and seven at the time, give back participation trophies. On the *Steve Harvey Show*, Harrison explained that he's an old-school parent, and that he told his boys that he was very proud of them for the effort. He then very patiently explained to them that you must earn things in life, because nothing is given to you. He didn't mock or ridicule them. He merely stated some basic facts about life. This is a lesson that will most likely bode well for both of his children.[1]

Harrison himself didn't have an easy road in his life, or making it in the NFL. He was the youngest of 14 children and was always fighting for basic necessities at home. Listed on the Steelers roster at 6'0" tall (many say he's really 5'9"), he's very undersized for an NFL linebacker. In fact, he wasn't drafted by any pro teams out of college and was cut seven times before he made the roster of an NFL team.

Harrison learned the approach he took with his kids from his parents. This same approach helped him overcome great obstacles to now be considered one of the greatest Steelers ever. He's had a wonderful 15-year NFL career so far and played in three Super Bowls, winning two. In fact, he still has the record for the longest interception return, 100 yards, for a touchdown.

In the interview, Steve Harvey, whose father, coincidentally, was a coal miner, explained that in his childhood he didn't get participation trophies either. And when he didn't get one, it just made him work that much harder. Harvey ended his point by stating that life doesn't give you anything; you must earn what you get.[2]

Wise Insights From Coach Pat Summit

Overall, a good lesson regarding participation trophies from two incredibly successful individuals. I concur. Not winning a trophy taught me very valuable lessons and inspired me to work that much harder, and those trophies I earned after that hard work made me appreciate it even more.

Former Tennessee Volunteers women's basketball coach Pat Summit is a legend in the women's basketball world. Summit accrued 1,098 career wins, the most in NCAA basketball history. She was quite the motivator and was known for many inspirational quotes. My favorite of hers is, "Losing strengthens you. It reveals your weaknesses so you can find them."[3] Sage advice, Coach Summit. Rest in peace.

Overprotective Society

A common title we now often hear is "helicopter parents." These are parents who are overprotective and who take excessive interest in their children. Oftentimes, these parents shield their kids from the learnings that accompany failure, hard work, leadership.

In speaking with Barry Alvarez, he said: "We're becoming too protective. I think people protect their kids too much. Parents don't want their kids to face adversity. I tell parents, 'So why isn't your son or daughter coming to talk to me instead of you?' They feel they'll have repercussions with the coach. And I reply, so when they graduate from college and have their first difficulty at work, are you going to call the boss? Or is your son/daughter going to? Same thing is going to happen there. I tell parents, aren't they coming to University of Wisconsin to learn? This is part of the learning process. A lot of parents think their kids are going to be pro athletes. They ship them around, give them all these special treatments, and they aren't going to make it. Only 1% will make it. You've got to teach them how to 'grind' in the world. I think people miss the boat."

Graduates from the School of Hard Knocks

It appears that the school Pete Stracci talks about churned out some very impressive folks. Time and time again, throughout history, this school has proven its worth. As an example:

In 1944, thousands of 18-year-olds were landing on the beaches of Normandy during the D-Day Landings, eventually leading to the defeat of Nazi Germany during WWII. This generation, which faced horrible obstacles, ultimately became what is now called "The Greatest Generation."

Contrast that with today, when so many people, not just youths, struggle with day-to-day minor defeats and inconveniences. Negative emotional responses to every slight drive the day. I do a considerable amount of work with millennials and I've personally found a majority of them to be very positive, inquisitive and hard working. But let's face it, the meme is out there that many from this generation are not as adept at facing difficulties as previous generations. Per one of the most famous and successful millennials, Mark Zuckerberg: *"The biggest risk is not taking any risk ... in a world that is changing really quickly, the only strategy that is guaranteed to fail is not taking risks."* [4]

The bottom line, regardless of your generation or background, is that rational, reasoned responses save the day, not irrational, emotionally charged ones. The willingness to face adversity is vital to our growth as human beings.

To Succeed in Life, You Must Accept & Acknowledge

There are two base elements in successfully dealing with adversity. First, you must accept that adversity is NOT going away. You can't avoid it. Despite how hard you may try to avoid it, something will occur such as a difficult person, a hurricane, an illness, the loss of a job or loved one, etc. The bottom line is this: you cannot hide from life; it will occur without your permission. So doesn't it make sense to prepare yourself for when adversity, big, or small, does strike?

Secondly, once you accept that adversity is going to happen, you must then acknowledge that it is meant for us to evolve as human beings. Therefore, avoiding it stunts our development. There are no safe spaces. Life won't allow it. Accepting that adversity will happen, and acknowledging that it is meant for us to grow, creates a foundational mindset not only for overcoming it, but possibly for profiting from it.

BOOK TERMINOLOGY
Adversity—Webster's defines adversity as *a state or instance of serious difficulty or misfortune.* Adversity could vary from tragic life-changing events to a minor delay in something. Essentially, adversity runs the gamut for different people. Personally, I don't like a lot of quick changes in my life. I need time to process, so such instances can be stressful for me and create a sense of adversity. Others embrace change, so it's not an issue for them. For that reason, we'll let you define your own meaning for adversity whether it's taking a risk, making a change, confronting a difficult boss, colleague, or customer.

What Lens Do You Use When You Face Adversity?

Someone I greatly admire and who highly motivates me is Chad Hymas. In 2001, Chad was involved in a serious accident. His life changed in an instant when a 2,000-pound bale collapsed on him, leaving him a quadriplegic. However, Chads dreams were not paralyzed that day, and he's leveraged this tragic accident into an opportunity to serve others. His list of accomplishments is quite impressive: he is one of the youngest ever to receive the Council of Peers Award for Excellence (CPAE) and to be inducted into the prestigious National Speaker Hall of Fame. He is president of his own communications company and best-selling author of a book on his life story called *Doing What Must be DONE—Even limitations can be used to make life BETTER!* He is a recognized world-class wheelchair athlete. In 2003, Chad set a world record by wheeling his chair from Salt Lake City to Las Vegas (513 miles).

As part of this book, Chad was gracious enough to carve out time from his busy schedule to speak about his view of adversity. Simply put, he says adversity depends upon the lens you choose to view it through. If you choose to look at adversity as a negative thing, then it will be negative for you. If you choose to look at it through the lens of something positive, it can be a positive thing. Chad uses his story to inspire and motivate thousands of people every year. He travels as many as 300,000 miles a year, captivating and motiving thousands with his insights. In using his own personal situation to help others, he has definitely chosen to view adversity through a positive lens. In fact, Chad recently posted a quote on his Facebook site that read, "Sometimes when you're in a dark place, you think you've been buried, but actually you've been planted." That's adversity being viewed through that positive lens.

Life is Difficult—Insights from Author Dr. Scott Peck

Regarding the school of hard knocks, I will share a great insight from one of my favorite books. In Dr. Scott Peck's outstanding *The Road Less Traveled*, the first few sentences say:

> *"Life is difficult. This is a great truth, one of the greatest truths. It is a great truth because once we truly see this truth, we transcend it. Once we truly know that life is difficult—once we truly understand and accept it—then life is no longer difficult. Because once it is accepted, the fact that life is difficult no longer matters."*

I love his insight here, as it speaks to a basic necessity for success in life. Life is not easy or fair, so don't expect it to be. Another truth is that adversity is going to occur in our lives, regardless of how much we try to avoid it. Two key takeaways as we move forward: Life isn't fair, and adversity is meant to be.

SAGE INSIGHTS

Adversity is simply a fact of life. No one manages to slide through life without adversity, difficulties, or roadblocks, and if they do, they aren't living life to its fullest potential! When initially faced with adversity, I might heave a deep sigh because really, who wants more difficulties in life?! Go ahead and acknowledge the adversity for what it is and have that moment. For some people, maybe it may need to be more than a moment, but you can't get carried away with it. Acknowledge and move on. Figure out what Plan B is, and if you need to really have control, figure out Plan C as well. But bottom line, everyone at some point in their life will face adversity. Know this and know that you can survive and be stronger than ever.

- Candace Andersson, Medical Sales Liaison in the Pharmaceutical Industry

Adversity is *Meant to Be*

Every day provides us with examples that adversity and problems are supposed to occur in our lives in order to help us evolve into better beings if we are aware. Take these examples:

One of my favorite metaphors on how Mother Nature proves adversity is meant for us to grow is how diamonds are essentially birthed from a piece of coal. The piece of coal becomes a diamond only after years of pressure. Being that I love motivational quotes, one of my favorites speaks to this point, and I'll repeat it from earlier in this book. Per the old Chinese proverb, *"The gem cannot be perfected without friction, nor can man be perfected without trials."*

Look at that as a metaphor for our lives. Just as coal evolves into a diamond under pressure, our trials can evolve us into something magnificent.

The same goes with heat and steel. Steel is given strength by heating it to an upper critical temperature and then quickly cooling it. This process is known as tempering. Heating steel to a lower critical temperature allows the crystalline structure to form austenite. This allotrope is not quite as hard as quenched steel, but it is nevertheless less prone to shattering.

Our problems shape and strengthen us. Without the heat, we lose some strength, become fragile, and possibly crack under pressure.

Another example is the Garnacha grape. This grape is found in Spain and ripens in an incredibly harsh environment. It is known to produce some of the finest wine in the world. The conditions where this grape flourishes include rocky soil, high elevation, and old vines. Due to the high elevation, the grape faces intense sunlight. These conditions lead to the grapes developing a thicker skin, which creates a greater concentration of fruit in the wine, hence the incredible flavor.[5]

Just like adversity, difficulties "thicken our skin." The thick skin of this grape, derived from adversity, enhances its flavor, allowing us, and the grape, to evolve into what was meant to be.

In *God's Word for Gardeners Bible*, Shelley S. Cramm explores how gardening provides many practical and relevant lessons in life. She says, "My favorite lesson from the garden is that what may seem like adversities are inherent pains to the process of growth ... and growth always has a good, fruitful outcome." In the book, she also says:

> *"This reality that we will be pruned or cut back from time to time is evident in the grapevine metaphor. There is probably no plant in greater need of drastic pruning than a grapevine! It is no accident*

that this is the plant featured in John 15, also that God's pet name for Israel was grapevine ... as in, 'News alert, people, you will be cut back now and again!' I am completely captivated by the insight that horticultural metaphors give, and the emotional strength, understanding, and guidance to endure prunings and hardships." [6]

Sage insights indeed, and yet another example that *"Nature proves ... adversity is meant to be."*

A Lesson from Herefords ... Nature Proves *Adversity is Meant to Be*

In a Facebook post, Chad Hymas relayed this story about cattle, namely Herefords. A Wyoming cowboy was once asked what the greatest lesson was that he'd learned from his experiences ranching. His reply was thus:

"The Herefords taught me one of life's most important lessons," he replied. "We used to breed cattle for a living, but the winter storms would come and kill 'em off. It would take a terrible toll on the herd.

"Time and time again, after a cold winter storm, we'd find most of our cattle piled up against the fences, dead as doornails. They would turn their backs to the icy wind and slowly drift downward until the fences stopped them. There, they just piled up and died. But the Herefords were different than that," he continued. "They would head straight into the wind and slowly walk the other way until they came to the upper boundary fence where they stood, facing the storm. We always found our Herefords alive and well. They saved their hides by facing the storm."

Our Mental Development Proves *Adversity is Meant to Be*

Look at the way our educational system functions. For us to grow to the next level of learning, our teachers gave us problems to solve and tests to pass. They didn't call them "easies." They were called problems, and we needed to learn to solve them in order to advance in our learning. That pressure or testing, and the challenging work of studying, allowed us to evolve in our educational and mental capacities.

Our Physical Development Proves *Adversity is Meant to Be*

Let's think about our physical development and growth. Do we become stronger by lifting heavier or lighter weights? Do we gain endurance by running with the wind in our face, or the wind at our back? Obviously, we grow stronger by lifting heavier weights and by running into the wind or up a hill—*against resistance.*

The same goes for any competitive venue. The tougher the competition or resistance, the more we learn and grow and the stronger we become. Truth be told, in my many years of athletics, I thoroughly enjoyed the tougher challenges more than the easier ones, win or lose. An easy win in football wasn't nearly as fun as the close game or the battle. Winning brought the sense of accomplishment, of overcoming a challenge.

On the flipside, defeat, albeit not desired, always provided an even greater sense of learning and a chance to grow and improve, if I chose to look at it in that manner. Sometimes this is easier said than done, but one thing is for sure: as I look back at my losses and difficulties, I learned a thing or two of great value and grew a ton. Adversity and defeat had their purpose, which was to make me a better person and prepare me for both the successes and failures that lay ahead. If you learn to look at victories, and more importantly, defeats, as a chance to grow, you will also prevail. In addition, if you gave it your best effort, losses aren't as difficult. You tried your best; you fought hard. You left it on the field, as they say. In other words, you have no regrets, which, in my opinion, is significantly more difficult than failing or losing.

History Proves *Adversity is Meant to Be*

Many of the greatest leaders and most successful people in the history of our world overcame great obstacles. These difficulties provided the path to their becoming outstanding, influential leaders. Here are just a few of my favorite examples that come to mind:

- **Winston Churchill**—My all-time personal favorite, and possibly the most influential man, who helped lead the defeat of Nazi Germany in World War II. He was indeed an accomplished man, leader, and great orator, but it all didn't come easily. Churchill faced many challenges throughout his life, some of which were quite devastating. He had a lisp. His father despised him and thought his son was doomed to failure. He was accident-prone and a poor student in school.

  In addition, he suffered great failure and setbacks throughout his political career—perhaps the biggest was his being blamed for

Britain's tragic defeat in the Battle of Gallipoli. However, he didn't let adversity deter him. He leveraged those difficulties and failures, as he knew they were stepping stones preparing him to become a great leader. Bottom line: Churchill's defeats prepared him for his greatest success, being the face of the opposition to Adolph Hitler. He could arguably be declared the greatest leader the world ever produced during one of its most dangerous and trying times.

- **Abraham Lincoln**—How many times have you heard the old stories about how often Abe Lincoln failed before becoming the 16th president of the United States? He failed at business, failed during several political runs for office, and experienced nervous breakdowns and familial deaths. All of these setbacks didn't deter him, as he ultimately became one of the greatest American presidents, and most importantly, preserved the Union during the Civil War.

- **Helen Keller**—Born deaf and blind, Keller ended up hugely successful despite her disabilities. She is one of the most inspirational women in history, known for overcoming great adversity to become an advocate for the suffrage movement.

- **Michael Jordan**—Quite possibly the greatest basketball player to ever play the game, he was cut by his eighth grade coach. Jordan often marvels at how many times he failed, as these failures always led to greater success. According to Jordan,

"I've missed more than 9,000 shots in my career. I've lost almost 300 games. Twenty-six times, I've been trusted to take the game-winning shot and missed. I've failed over and over and over again in my life. And that is why I succeed."

In addition, Jordan also believes not trying is even worse than failing, per this quote, *"I can accept failure. Everyone fails at something. But I can't accept not trying."* It also appears he thinks regret is far worse than failure, something I wholeheartedly agree with.[7]

Lastly, he looks at adversity as a challenge: *"Obstacles don't have to stop you. If you run into a wall, don't turn around and give up. Figure out how to climb it, go through it, or work around it."* Sage advice from one of the greatest athletes of all time.[8]

- **J.K. Rowling**—Author of the wildly popular *Harry Potter* books, at a Harvard commencement speech she said this of adversity:

"You might never fail on the scale I did, but some failure in life is inevitable. It is impossible to live without failing at something, unless you live so cautiously that you might as well not have lived at all—in which case, you fail by default. Failure gave me an inner security that I had never attained by passing examinations. Failure taught me things about myself that I could have learned no other way. I discovered that I had a strong will, and more discipline than I had suspected; I also found out that I had friends whose value was truly above the price of rubies. The knowledge that you have emerged wiser and stronger from setbacks means that you are, ever after, secure in your ability to survive. You will never truly know yourself, or the strength of your relationships, until both have been tested by adversity. Such knowledge is a true gift, for all that it is painfully won, and it has been worth more than any qualification I ever earned." [9]

- **Denzel Washington**—The Academy Award-nominated actor recently gave an incredibly inspiring speech on adversity. I saw the video on Facebook of him speaking during a commencement speech, walking through all the obstacles he had to overcome to ultimately achieve his goal of being one of our greatest actors. His final message to the students was as follows:

"So, members of the class of 2011, this is your mission. When you leave the friendly confines of Philly, never be discouraged. Never hold back. Give everything you've got. And when you fall throughout life, and maybe even tonight, after a few too many glasses of champagne, remember this: fall forward." [10]

- **Rocky Bleier**—The beloved Pittsburgh Steeler running back overcame a physically challenging Vietnam War wound and his small size to become one of the stars during the Steelers' four Super Bowl wins in the 1970s. Initially, he was considered a longshot to even make the team. Those chances worsened upon his return from the war. Doctors had to remove over 100 pieces of shrapnel from his right foot and leg. After much rehab, and a gracious Rooney family (owners of the Steelers franchise), Bleier recovered, and the rest is history. He is now a successful businessman and motivational speaker.[11]

- **Oprah Winfrey**—In her youth, Winfrey was demoted from her job as a news anchor because she "wasn't suited" for television. In 2017, she made Forbes' List of America's Richest Self-Made Women. Her net worth was listed at $2.9 billion. Not bad for someone who was supposedly not suited for television. Imagine if she had let that comment deter her. Thank God for her, and so many other people who have gained value from her successful ventures.[12]

- **Steve Jobs**—When he was 30 years old, he was left devastated and depressed after being unceremoniously removed from the company he'd started. At the time of his death in 2011, his net worth was estimated at $11 billion.[13]

- **Walt Disney**—This incredible man, who positively touched the lives of countless children and their families, was fired from a newspaper for "lacking imagination and having no original ideas." Let's remind that person of what Disney's wife later said about Walt's imagination. During Epcot's opening ceremony, a reporter asked Disney's wife, Lillian, to comment on what Walt would have thought of Epcot, had he lived to see it. Her response was a classic testament to his visionary imagination, as she simply replied, *"He did see it. That's why it's here."* [14]

This is just a very short list of famous people who faced and overcame many obstacles prior to accomplishing incredible things that positively influenced the lives of millions of people. Every single day, many people face similar, often greater, odds and overcome them to become great in their own right. The ability to experience, face, and overcome obstacles is one of the greatest experiences in life.

Personal Testament

My life is a testament that true growth occurs when adversity is faced and overcome. My greatest learnings have all come during my toughest times. One of the most memorable and influential occurred during what I refer to as *"the summer from hell."*

READER CALL TO ACTION

1.   List 3-5 Key Takeaways/Learnings from Chapter 1.

2.   How do you currently view adversity? In a negative light, a positive light, and why? Can you connect dots to how an adverse situation actually ended up benefitting you?

3.   List 5-7, or more of your favorite quotes about overcoming adversity.

4.   Who are some of your personal inspirations or heroes who've overcome hardships to become successful? What is their story, and why does it inspire you? What did you learn from them that can assist you?

CHAPTER 2

THE SUMMER FROM HELL

The obstacle is the path.

~

-Zen Proverb-

The First Shoe Drops

It was a beautiful spring day outside the Phi Gamma Delta fraternity house at Allegheny College in Meadville, Pennsylvania. My fraternity brothers were throwing a football and laughing and taunting each other, as usual. It was a perfect day, beautiful weather, hanging out with my best friends. Next year, I would begin my last year of college and then enter the real world. I had only great vibes, optimism, and anticipation for the year ahead. Then came the call.

Steve, We've Lost Our House

I was outside talking with my best friend, Gordon, when another friend called out from a window, "Steve, you have a phone call!" It was my mother. My mother *never* called the fraternity house, let alone in the middle of the afternoon. I was immediately concerned.

I heard the strain in her voice as soon as I picked up the phone. She'd been crying, and her voice was shaky. "Steve, I want you to know before you hear it from someone else that we've lost our house."

The first thing I thought about was Steve's Fruit Market, our family business. Had something happened to the business that had caused financial strain and forced us out of the house? Or had my father made a bad financial investment I wasn't aware of? Then my mother told me what had really happened on that fateful day in western Pennsylvania.

Like Something Out of a Horror Movie

The night before, my parents were relaxing and watching TV after a long, hard day of work. Around 11:00 p.m., they started hearing strange noises, creaks, and cracks. We were all familiar with the normal sounds of a house settling, but these were entirely different, my mother said, and quite frightening. As they inspected the house, they saw cracks streaking from the corner of the bedroom window to the corner of the wall. Along with the cracks came a gritty, sandy sound. My mother said it was like something out of a horror movie. They immediately got out of the house and spent the night at my grandmother's home, which was located on our property.

The next day, they entered the house and saw that the foundation was cracked down the middle and had fallen at least three feet between the living room and dining room. The living room curtains were hanging at an angle on the picture window. As my parents soon found out, this is a common occurrence in western Pennsylvania. Turned out, our house had been built on top of a mining room. The collapse, similar to a sinkhole, was caused by mine subsidence, due to the coal mines which had at one time been below our house's foundation. We had no idea!

Since the house was on a slab and had no basement, it couldn't be repaired by lifting it and filling the void underneath. The federal government was responsible for underground repair with mine subsidence, so tearing down the house and rebuilding was the only choice. What made matters worse was that our homeowners insurance didn't cover mine subsidence. Such insurance had to be purchased from the state, which my parents hadn't realized. Most of our furniture and belongings were rescued, but the home that my parents had worked so hard for, where we had built our memories, had to be torn down. To add insult to injury, my parents had only two more mortgage payments to make before the home would have been theirs.

The only option available was provided by the state of Pennsylvania: if we rebuilt on the same property, they'd allow a small, low-interest loan. My father accepted the offer. My parents soon moved into a one-bedroom apartment as they dealt with the devastating loss of our home and the stress of building a new one. It was quite an emotional time for us, but that was just the beginning.

The Second Shoe Drops

Little did I realize, there were more tests to come for my family and me that summer. A few weeks after our house collapsed, I came home for summer vacation. As with every other break from college, I worked in my father's produce market. I enjoyed the work. I liked learning new things and the interactions I had with people. It wasn't always that way. In fact, I initially hated it, but it grew on me. As the years passed, my dad taught me about the business, giving me additional responsibilities, and teaching me how to run a business. More importantly, the experience helped me mature. By the time the summer from hell came around, the only thing he hadn't taught me about the business was how he calculated profit margins.

About a week after I came home, my father, who was already under a great deal of stress, began complaining about chest pains. We all grew very concerned. It was then that my father taught me about profit margins.

Thank God he did. The very next day, he was admitted into the hospital. A calcium deposit caused by his rheumatoid arthritis had punctured his lung and caused it to collapse, so he would be out of commission for some time. So, there we were: a collapsed house, my dad laid up in the hospital, and my mom couldn't quit her job to help because we had to pay for the hospitalization. How were we going to make it?

My Education in the School of Hard Knocks

As I look back, that summer may have been the best thing that ever happened to me. At the time, I thought my head was going to explode. I'd never felt so much stress, fear, and anxiety in my life. It was intense. However, with the stress came something else: a sense of confidence. Instead of responding with complete emotion, I cleared my head, thought logically about the situation, and realized I had options. I had a strong foundation to fall back on, including everything my father had taught me about the business and the experience I'd gained from working there and in other jobs. It also allowed me the opportunity to put to use some of my economic understanding in a real-world environment. Even my years of experience as an athlete played a role. I realized that I knew what to do, and that I could do it.

As he recovered from his illness, my father spent most of his time overseeing the rebuilding of our house while I ran the store. I did everything from ordering, pricing, working the register, merchandising and promotion, to managing the staff. Although wet behind the ears, I ran the store for the entire summer and learned a lot about both business and myself. That year turned out to be one of the most successful years of the business. By the end of summer, my dad was fully recovered, the new house was built, and I was due to return to college with quite a huge feather in my cap.

The Best School I Ever Attended

That summer's events were among the most influential experiences in my life. I grew emotionally and mentally that summer, and I became a man overnight. I faced additional setbacks that summer; the biggest letdown was that I didn't play football my senior year in college because I was running the store and couldn't prepare for summer camp. That letdown turned out to be such a blessing. When I started interviewing for jobs at the end of my senior year, the experience of successfully running my family's business was what interested most potential employers, rather than my grades or what I'd studied.

By the time I graduated, I had five job offers. I eventually took the job that changed my life in many ways. While there, I met the most important mentor in my life, Santo Laquatra. At the time, Santo was Director of Training & Development at Beecham Products. He was, and still is, a massive influence in my life.

The obstacles I faced that summer were, without a doubt, what led me to bigger and better things and brought me to where I am today. In hindsight, I realize that nearly all the difficulties I have faced—from sports, other jobs, or life in general—albeit painful, have led to better things.

SAGE INSIGHTS

The trick for me to remain positive during times of adversity is to remember that adversity is interchangeable with advantage. Every instance of adversity that we face provides us with experience and knowledge. The more adversity we have, the more experience and knowledge we gain. And as we accrue more experience and knowledge, we create advantages for ourselves—advantages against our competition, advantages against new forms of adversity, and so on.

- Justin Moore, Attorney, former military officer, founder and CEO of non-profit organization

The Fruits from The School of Hard Knocks

I consider myself very successful. I'm a speaker, trainer, and coach to some of the country's biggest companies. And, well, heck, you're reading my book! My non-work life is also pretty enjoyable. Most people who consider themselves successful (and everyone has their own definition of success) can point to at least one specific incident or person that helped shape them. Mine is the summer from hell. The adversity I faced and overcame helped me mature and made my family and me stronger. Did we seek it out and enjoy it? Absolutely not. Nevertheless, it made us a closer family and transformed me into a stronger person.

Just like building a house, the foundation is poured first. Without a solid underpinning, the structure will topple over. The same went for me that summer. Prior experiences had provided me with a strong foundation that sustained me so I didn't crumble under stress like our house did. And that summer from hell further strengthened that foundation for my future. Who would have thought that our house situation would prove to be a perfect metaphor for me, my life, and this book?

A Mystery is Solved

In hindsight, I realize that my experiences prepared me for that summer. However, what was occurring with me at that time was a mystery. One of the things that stuck with me for many years was how I stayed calm when the burden of running the family business was laid at my feet. After the initial shock of realizing this new reality, a sudden calm rushed over me. I knew in part that my father and other events had prepared me for this very moment. However, it wasn't until recently that I realized that there was more at work with my psyche than I first realized. There was a reason why I didn't panic and remained calm. There was a reason I knew I had options and didn't let my emotions run amok. I learned exactly why a few years ago from my kickboxing instructor Eric Parker, someone who also knows how to grind.

READER CALL TO ACTION

1. List 3-5 Key Takeaways/Learnings from Chapter 2.

2. Do you have a "summer from hell" moment and epiphany (feel free to list several, if relevant)?

If so, what was the situation, what were the outcomes, and what did you learn? What can you still learn from it? How has it been a benefit for you (i.e. tangible, or simply a lesson/experience to strengthen you)? Would you do anything different in hindsight?

PART II
THE JOURNEY OF SELF-DISCOVERY

CHAPTER 3

BUILDING A FOUNDATION AND ENVIRONMENT TO GRIND

My father used to say to me, whenever you get into a jam, whenever you get into a crisis or emergency ... become the calmest person in the room and you'll be able to figure your way out of it.

~

-Rudy Giuliani-

Grind

As I contemplate the high success rate of the people from my hometown, my mind wanders to how they became so adept at facing and overcoming adversity. What was the mindset that led to them overcoming such hardships? And what was the thinking at that time, which seems to be lacking today? In Barry Alvarez's words, how did they learn to grind?

I strongly suspect a great deal of it had to do with how they viewed adversity. As Chad Hymas might say, what lens was adversity viewed through? They didn't panic or quit. They sought the upside. They knew their goals, and difficulties didn't deter them. They knew they had options in America, so they remained focused. Hence, their responses to difficulties were rational, not emotional. There is also something more that I learned recently which may provide some answers for why they succeeded, despite tough odds. I think that a great deal of it had to do with what part of the brain people are accessing when under stress and facing adversity.

A Valuable Lesson from My Kickboxing Coach

My former Muay Thai and Brazilian jiu-jitsu instructor, Eric Parker, taught me about this. Parker trains Mixed Martial Arts (MMA) athletes in a program called Wintensity—The Psychology of Combat and Effective Mental Preparation. The premise of this program is creating the right mindset before and during a fight to ensure success. Parker enlightens participants of his program about the need for successful fighters to access cortex thinking by learning how to utilize the logical reasoning part of the brain, rather than the emotional side, otherwise known as the limbic system. The ability to access the cortex takes experience, training, and work. This fighter's philosophy can easily be applied to facing and overcoming life's adversities.

What Part of the Brain Are You Accessing?

Eric Parker not only believes in his program, he has lived it for most of his life. He's been training in martial arts since he was six years old. He is a former marine, 10-year veteran police officer, eight-year SWAT team member, SWAT section leader and instructor, and five-year canine handler. He is also an undefeated Muay Thai amateur fighter with a 12-0 record. He is currently vice president and regional manager of a large private bank based in New York. He's quite an accomplished individual, and that didn't happen by accident.

Prior to developing Wintensity, Parker was a nationally certified tactical instructor for firearms, patrol rifles, chemical agents, less-lethal munitions, and impact weapons. One of his core training elements was understanding how the brain and body process and function under critical incident stress and, more importantly, what survival actions a person should take during such times. With this understanding, officers are able to effectively deal with stressful situations by using the afore-mentioned cortex thinking. And Parker has practical experience with his approach.

Walking the Walk

Several years ago, Parker was leading a SWAT team raid when a gunfight broke out. Almost immediately, he was badly wounded through his left forearm and his training gave him the presence of mind to respond accordingly. He had been returning fire with the shotgun he was carrying, but lost the use of his left arm when wounded and could no longer use the shotgun to continue firing. Instead of giving up, Parker switched weapons and began to return fire with his handgun. Then, running out of ammo, he reloaded one-handed. He credits his training to not only staying in the fight but, more importantly, to fighting for his survival. His training and his understanding of the following contributed to his success:

- How the human brain functions under the stress of combat
- How the stress of combat directly affects physical abilities and performance
- How to successfully handle anxiety, stress, pain, and fear
- How to build brain training into your physical training in order to reach your potential, physically and mentally
- What to expect from yourself in a real-world encounter
- How to develop a true non-quitting spirit

The process he learned and still teaches not only helped him operate at peak performance under duress, but also saved his life. He is living proof that his approach works.

The Limbic System vs. the Cortex

Parker explains that we have two essential parts of our brain, the limbic system and the cortex. The limbic system, often referred to as the emotional brain, contains the following responses to danger and stress. All of these are natural responses, but not part of a predictable cognitive process:

- Freeze
- Flight
- Fight

When people are in such an emotional state, there is an adrenaline rush and if not handled properly, it can cause people to fall into the freeze, flight, fight mode. This may lead to unclear, irrational thinking which hinders the ability to face and overcome difficulties. In addition, when people fall into that emotional state, it is highly unlikely that it can be reversed in the moment and can instead often escalate. You most likely will not be able to pull out of that emotional state until the adverse event is over and can be properly processed.

BOOK TERMINOLOGY

Emotional Response—For this book, emotional response is defined as freeze/flight/fight. I'm not saying emotions are totally bad. As an example, sadness is an emotion and it's good to mourn a loss. There are other such examples too. However, a reaction to adversity that hinders you and stops you from taking productive action in the face of adversity is not beneficial.

Speed of Adversity—Emotional Responses

This need to understand the emotional state is especially important in this day and age. As stated in the beginning of this book, adversity is hitting us at a pace like never before and that is not likely to stop. In fact, I believe that speed will be intensified due to the ever-evolving world of technology and the change its driving. As such, it is very important to recognize the importance of not responding emotionally to adversity. We're getting hit faster and harder, so self-awareness is key.

Meanwhile, the cortex is the part of the brain where reason and logic exist. It is necessary for:

- Formulating and planning

- Drawing upon lessons learned from those plans and experiences

- Full use of our physical, analytical, and decision-making skills

Unlike the limbic system, cortical cells mature, and cortical thoughts gain the ability to process at higher levels and in more complex situations. Therefore, you can learn as you progress, and if you are functioning in the cortex, you can apply these lessons learned. Essentially, if your brain is operating in the cortex, you will be able to maintain cognitive thought even under stress.

The key point of Parker's training is this: To be successful during times of stress, it's essential to **prevent the transfer authority** from the cortex to the limbic system (which is the natural human response to pressure and stress) to ensure that your responses to the stress are dealt with logically, not emotionally (freeze, fight, or flight). It is important to reference back to the training you've received or similar situations in which you've had success.

SAGE INSIGHTS

Remember, there are varying degrees of challenging situations, each one with a different level of physical, mental, and emotional impact. The immediate response can be anger, sadness, grief, etc. Adversity is a reaction based on our perception of a situation and that negative reaction is based on a story we tell ourselves about the event or the messenger and whether the story is true. The inner critic is a master at hammering us. After the initial issue, stepping back and stopping to breathe and think so you can then choose to respond helps move things along in order to see the bigger picture, whether it a sport performance or a business deal.

- Barrie Pressley, RN, CPC & Certified Master Coach at Zone Mastery

Putting it Into Action

I recently had an email exchange with a pediatric neuropsychologist where she broke it all down in laymen terms. To paraphrase, essentially, when the body experiences shock, it triggers the limbic system to produce different levels of hormones (HPA). The limbic system helps us to regulate our stress response as well as form and access memories, especially those with an emotional component. So, when you perceive a stressful or adverse event, part of what helps you regulate your ability to cope with it (or not) are the emotionally-laden memories of similar past experiences, which are activated by the limbic system.

The key is to "teach the cortex" how to perceive and cope with a threat or stressor, so it can then allow the limbic system to inhibit the body's natural hormonal stress reaction. Thinking in the cortex can monitor the hormones and minimize or eliminate the emotional response. So, the ability to stay in the cortex is imperative.

Simply put, you can fall back on training or past experiences to slow hormone production and limit the limbic response of freeze, flight, and fight. You can, in turn, stay in the cortex to logically view the situation and fall back on your training and experiences to address the situation or solve the problem. If you don't access the cortex and instead stay in the limbic system, the scenario may snowball and the situation could worsen. At that point, it may be nearly impossible to convert out of the difficulty.

What Part of the Brain is Being Accessed?

So how do we know which part of our brain is being accessed? When a human perceives danger and believes he/she has options to deal with that danger, meaning they've been there before, physically and psychologically, then the human brain will retain function in the cortex. On the other hand, when a human perceives danger and he/she believes there are no options (due to lack of experience and control) to deal with the danger, or when a human is in a significantly emotional state, the human brain will transfer authority from the cortex to the limbic system, making the options freeze, flight or fight.

BOOK TERMINOLOGY

Options—The realization that your response to adversity does not have to be solely emotional. Based on learnings, experience, and/or a willingness to learn from adverse situations, you realize you have "options" to respond rationally, NOT emotionally. The more experiences and options you have at your disposal, the more arsenal you have to effectively deal with adversity.

A Serious Matter

According to Parker, 33% of police officers killed in the line of duty by felonious assault (shot, stabbed, intentionally run over by car) did nothing to prevent their own deaths, despite their training and weapons. Why didn't they respond? Because they were stuck in the limbic system. They were shocked because they had never truly prepared themselves for a deadly force encounter, felt they were out of options, and had no experience with the situation or control over the outcome. A transfer of authority from the cortex to the limbic system occurred and they got stuck on freeze, flight, or fight.

Housed in the limbic system is the amygdala, the part of the brain where fear and anger reside. This leads to the old adage that you should never make a crucial decision when angry. Although you're thinking, you are not thinking at the same logical level as you would when in the cortex, where reason and logic exist. You're thinking emotionally, rather than rationally.

As you transfer to the limbic system, it's hard to access the cortex, primarily because stress levels compound in the limbic system. The ability to access and stay in the cortex is what saved Parker's life the night of the gunfight. In layman's terms, he stayed calm, cool, collected, and he relied on his training to effectively defend himself and escape a deadly situation. If he had let himself be in a highly emotional state and operated in the limbic system, he might have responded via freeze, flight, or fight, with devastating results.

SAGE INSIGHTS

My maternal grandfather worked hard his entire life to raise a family. Around his 59th birthday, he was severely injured in an explosion and carried his son, daughter-in-law, and their kids from the scene to safety. He later died from the wounds. His ability to search, decide, and execute a plan ensured their survival. One casualty (his own) ensured the lives of the group.

-Brian Petrucci, Corporate Training & Development Manager at Acme Construction Supply (Born and raised in Burgettstown, Pa.)

Accessing the Cortex

Part of Parker's past training with police officers, and now current training of MMA fighters, focuses on approaches that revolve around improving access to cortex thinking. His approach is based heavily on the Skinner box approach and Gestalt Theory. These are two psychological approaches that enable us to understand how people function in given scenarios.

The Skinner Box

The Skinner box produces basic, trained responses in a repetitive, tightly controlled environment. Developed by B.F. Skinner, a Skinner box is a chamber that contains a bar or key that an animal presses or manipulates to get food or water as a type of reinforcement. The Skinner box is also equipped with a device to record each response provided by the animal, as well as the unique schedule of reinforcement that the animal has been assigned.

Parker's use of the Skinner box approach with MMA is repetitive exercises (like boxing, kicking, or jiu-jitsu moves) that ultimately become second nature. These exercises are as basic as learning to throw a punch properly or learning a more advanced striking combination (basic strikes with both hands and feet, possibly with knees and elbows). Then, when the opportunity presents itself in an actual competitive scenario, the fighter relies on what he/she has learned through repetition. In other words, the foundational skills for success have been laid.

Foundational Skill Development

Essentially, I do the same thing in my coaching and training business. Most of my programs have foundational skills attached in the form of a process. As an example, I have a 4-Step Consultative Selling Skills Process, a 4-Step Coaching Skills Process, and a 3-Step Process for Effective Communication. Each of these steps have skills that must be introduced, learned, and practiced. Basically, I'm using the same approach as Parker, employing a Skinner box to train on foundational elements for success in sales, management, and communication.

The same goes for anything in life—sports, education, home building, or medicine. For anyone to be successful in anything, it's very important to understand and master elements at the most rudimentary levels. A sturdy foundation is needed. Again, a great metaphor would be our family home. When the ground below our house caved in, it was because of a weak foundation.

Life's difficulties, our experiences, and possibly our skills, create that foundation. If we avoid them and/ or don't learn from them, we don't build the needed foundation to successfully maneuver through life when troubles come our way.

Gestalt Theory

Gestalt Theory involves understanding the laws of our abilities to acquire and maintain meaningful perceptions in what can be a chaotic environment, considering the object or event in its entirety. Simply, it is applying learned skills in a real-world environment. As Parker says, "train for your reality."

When applied to Parker's approach to training, it takes the fighter one step further from the repetition of throwing punches or kicks, putting all the basics together in a real-world environment with an opponent, also known as sparring. In addition to sparring, Parker sometimes throws other obstacles at a fighter to simulate real-world situations. As an example, he's been known to place eye patches on fighters so they are prepared if their vision is impaired due to swelling. They practice their basic skills (kickboxing basics = Skinner box) in a real-world scenario (sparring while one eye is covered = Gestalt Theory or "real-world scenario").

Parker's interpretation, from an MMA perspective, is if you don't train at the level you're expect to perform, or if you don't train in the environment where you're expect to perform, you should expect little transfer of ability. So, putting fighters in such situation prepares them for if/when it happens. Then, if it does, the fighter does not panic or slip into that emotional state. The fighter can respond rationally and logically, based on the training and experience. In other words, Parker has prepared the fighter to realize he/she has options when the proverbial "Sh*t hits the fan."

Real-World Environment Approach

This approach is also practiced by Iowa Hawkeye Quarterback Coach Ken O'Keefe. In an effort to get his quarterbacks to prepare for potential real-world environments, he tells them to practice throwing in adverse conditions. During the off-season, O'Keefe recommends his quarterbacks throw the football in a rainstorm, into the wind, and with the wind. It gets them used to the conditions Mother Nature might throw at them on game day. Their off-season experiences prepare them to effectively stay cool and function effectively in the face of adversity. When game day arrives and a rainstorm hits, his quarterbacks are prepared. They stay calm, cool, collected. After all, they've been here before and have the tools for coping and excelling.

Real-World Environment Training

Just as Parker and O'Keefe throw athletes into real-world scenarios to "get them used to it," I do the same with my workshop participants. I use case studies, roleplays, and simulated modules that are relevant to the world and issues my clients face. A selling scenario for a pharmaceutical sales rep will be very different from a real-estate agent, and those both will differ from a private banker interfacing with a client. It's imperative for me to clearly understand my clients' needs and the issues they face so I can build training modules relevant to them.

Learning skills without applying them to the specific world in which they are practiced greatly diminishes retention of learnings. It's practicing those basic skills in meaningful environments that drives both immediate use and success of learned skills, while driving long-term retention. That is my focus, point of differentiation, and a key to the success of my programs.

Succeeding During the Summer from Hell

As I think back to my summer from hell, I can't help but believe that Parker's approach applied to me. My first feeling was angst, but this soon turned to confidence. I firmly believe I operated in the cortex. The experiences of my past years working at the store provided me with self-assurance, and that foundation ignited my cortex. Without my prior experiences, my response could have easily been freeze, flight, or fight, and failure would probably have been the outcome.

Imagine the long-term effects of that scenario. What if I had failed my family during a time they needed me? If the market had shut down, we could have faced financial ruin. Instead, I stood at the plate and took responsibility for the situation. The benefits of that time still resonate with me to this very day. I had a foundation and learned to grind.

A Timely Testimonial

As I was writing this book, I had one of the highly successful people I interviewed write to me answering some questions I had posed to her regarding how she deals with adversity. She was a high-level manager in a large company who was considering leaving that job to purchase a growing franchise. She sent me this note, which perfectly encapsulates this process of accessing the cortex for a rational, reasoned response versus an emotional one.

> *Hello Steve ... you may not realize, but you were a blessing to me this week. I started reading through the franchise disclosure doc, which is about 300 pages, this week. I was feeling somewhat overwhelmed and was questioning my ability to run a business. While completing your adversity survey yesterday, I was reminded that I have been through so much change and adversity in my life and have always overcome it with success. I finished reading the franchise doc last night and felt so much more confident by the time I completed it. Thank you for asking for my own testimony ... who knew it would come just at the right time. It's a God thing!!! My husband and I*

meet with the regional development VP this afternoon. Keep you posted.

As you look at her note, it's clear that her response to this overwhelming decision and document was initially emotion-based (in her case, freeze/flight). Then she fell back on her past experiences and success and recognized she did indeed have options and could successfully run this business. In turn, her response ended up being rational and reasoned, not emotional. This is the perfect example of facing a challenge by staying in that logical, rational state of mind. This approach works!

Tony Robbins – Achieving a "Beautiful State"

In an online CNBC article called "Tony Robbins Reveals 3 Tips that Made Him a Megamillionaire," Robbins explains that the first step in being successful is managing your emotions. He teaches his clients to achieve what he calls a "beautiful state"—a perennially peaceful mood. That means never expecting anything from anyone, so instead of being disappointed when things don't work out, you'll remain the cool-headed leader who guides her team to victory amid adversity.

"Emotions are contagious," Robbins says. Panicked leaders are bound to transmit that panic to their employees, while leaders who have attained a beautiful state will help their businesses by passing on their positive mind-sets.[15]

Obviously Tony Robbins knows how to be successful and create success in other people. His point buttresses the argument made in this chapter and in this book. Be coolheaded in the face of difficulties and good things are sure to manifest themselves.

We Were Grinders

In the case of the families from my hometown, previous difficult experiences and obstacles enabled them to take logical, rational approaches to solving problems. When they faced difficulties, they dealt with them head-on and overcame, or, at the very least, learned from the experiences. They created a pathway of experiences that they could rely on and passed this type of thinking on to their children.

It's amazing, as I've been researching and writing this book over the years, how many times I heard the word "grind" used in describing people from this area, and what it means in the context of this book. I first heard it when I interviewed Barry Alvarez. Then, in a discussion with Eric Parker, who essentially said that he teaches his athletes the ability to *grind* during a fight. Then a friend, Justin Moore, a highly successful Tampa lawyer who grew up in the area as well, stated that people in that area are *grinders*. There is indeed something in this word and this area.

It may also explain why so many people today, especially youth, are struggling. They've been shielded from adversity and their experiences have not been allowed to manifest, so when the slightest degree of difficulty arises, they choose to give up or run away. Their training ground of experiences has either been taken away or minimized. Hence, they see no options and fall into an emotional response. They don't know how to grind. This book is about teaching them!

Self-Discovery

So now, hopefully, we've accepted the fact that adversity is not going to disappear from our lives. We know how our response to it can affect our lives and realize how our brain functions when it happens. Next, we will address how to become aware of when adversity happens and what it feels like, so we can address it purposefully. In the next several chapters, we will cover the following three valuable insights:

- **Behavioral Style Recognition**—I will introduce you to a popular, scientifically-valid assessment that you can use to understand and identify your behavioral style. Once you are aware of your style, you'll better understand your emotional triggers and responses. This knowledge will help you apply an appropriate, positive response to adversity.

- **Emotional Triggers**—Do certain people or events trigger emotional responses in you? We will investigate how this happens. By understanding your behavior style, you can gain awareness of the things that drive you toward an emotional response.

- **Emotional Responses**—Lastly, once you realize what your emotional response is, you can become more aware and make appropriate adjustments. When you're in the emotional state, how does it play with you? Freeze, fight, flight, or some combination of all three? If you know what sets you in that state and what it feels like, you can then respond accordingly in a positive manner.

Let's press forward and find out a bit about ourselves! Some more self-discovery insights, please.

READER CALL TO ACTION

1. List 3-5 Takeaways/Learnings from Chapter 3.

2. What is your typical response to adversity? Is it emotional (limbic system) or rational (cortex based)?

   - If emotional, is to freeze/fight/flight ... or some combination of the three?

3. When adversity hits, what are your first thoughts and actions?

4. What events do you consider "adverse"?

   - Change? Risk? Conflict?

   - Issues with people?

   - Not accomplishing goals?

5) List anything that comes to mind that you view as adversity.

CHAPTER 4

SELF-KNOWLEDGE AND SELF-AWARENESS ARE ESSENTIAL

Knowing yourself is the beginning of wisdom.

~

-Aristotle-

A Proactive and Productive Approach to Adversity

How can we learn to effectively handle adversity productively and rationally? After all our years of bad habits, creating a world of our own making, how can we change the trajectory of our lives and past learnings to begin better addressing adversity? And how does one go about finding those options that Eric Parker talks about?

After accepting that adversity is a part of life, then acknowledging that it's meant for us to evolve as human beings, we must know ourselves and what our reactions to adversity will be. After all, we are all very different. Our background, experiences, and genetic makeups, make us so, and that is a very good thing. We are each unique, so the first step is creating a high level of self-knowledge, self-awareness.

The more we know about ourselves, the more we will be able to predict how we'll respond to adversity both in things that may "set us off" and in what our response will be. Some people love and embrace change, some cannot stand it. An environment of drastic change may be seen by some as a challenge or an opportunity to grow, while others may see it as adversity. The key is to understand ourselves so we can handle adverse situations in our lives accordingly—rationally, logically, in a reasoned fashion, versus freeze, flight, fight.

Self-Knowledge and Self-Awareness are Essential

As mentioned, the speed of adversity is hugely important. Since we don't want to get stuck in that negative emotional state when adversity is hitting us so hard and fast, it's imperative that we gain self-knowledge to be aware and prepared for when adversity strikes.

The key is to begin building the skills for dealing with it by first understanding ourselves. How do we personally respond to adversity, especially when in that emotional state? Is our response to freeze? Flee? Fight? Some blended combination of those three? It's vital for us to recognize our response as well as what sets off our reactions, our triggers.

The deeper our understanding of our emotional triggers and responses, the more success we can have in dealing with adversity productively. At that point, we can seek solutions by either falling back on past positive experiences and/or creating new ones.

SAGE INSIGHTS

I know my response to adversity, and it depends on the situation. When it comes to money or work-related issues, I think I have a better handle than something having to do with family or health. My immediate reaction most times is to strongly feel some emotions [such as] anger, sadness, worry, and I generally allow myself to feel what I need to without lingering too long. Once I have a chance to sit with the difficulty, I am better able to assess it for what it is—not from a state of anxiety or fear, but from a place of acceptance.

- *Abby Goodwin, RYT Yoga Instructor*

The Foundation of Self-Knowledge—The Behavioral Assessment

One of the best ways to build self-knowledge to clearly understand yourself and your response to difficulties is to learn your respective behavioral style. You can do this by taking a behavioral-based assessment survey (sometimes also called personality assessments or introspective self-reports). There are many out there. Possibly the most well-known is the Myers-Briggs Type Indicator assessment. Most all are based on the Carl Jung theory and are quite good, with high predictive accuracy. I'm certified in Myers-Briggs and the DISC Behavioral Assessment.

Others you may have heard of include Social Styles, Colors, etc. However, I prefer DISC because of its accuracy, popularity, and its simplicity. I use this assessment in nearly all of my training and coaching programs. It's easy to understand and leverage for self-development and to improve interactions with others, both personally and professionally.

DISC and Self-Knowledge, Self-Awareness Connection

My premise is that to be successful in anything you do, you must first understand yourself, your behavior style, and how you communicate. Whether your need to overcome obstacles is professional—sales, management, leadership, or a team environment—and/or personal—relationship issues, financial burdens, health-related reasons, the more you know about yourself and your style, the more successful you will be at dealing with difficulties. The more you understand yourself, the richer your relationships and life become as well. The DISC Behavioral Assessment can help you become more knowledgeable and self-aware.

DISC Behavioral Assessment as a Foundation

In my consulting, coaching, and training business I prefer the DISC Behavioral Assessment because of its practicality. In fact, I'm a Certified Professional Behavioral Analyst through Target Training International, a major distributor of the DISC survey. DISC is simple to understand and use, both for self-development and understanding others. The TTI Success Insights version I use is also highly accurate. Scientifically supported, it's been around for many years, has a high predictive accuracy, and is universally accepted as a valid behavioral survey. We will use it as a basis for this book, leveraging DISC knowledge about ourselves to better understand our style, triggers, responses, and how to deal with others. Most importantly, it includes how that knowledge can help us better overcome adversity.

About DISC

First, let's provide some general insights about the DISC behavioral assessment. It's important to understand it, as we will build from this tool for the next few chapters. DISC behavioral assessment is:

- **Observable**—Meaning you can observe the behaviors in action. In other words, you can see the behaviors manifest in yourself and others.

- **Universal**—Meaning these four base styles are recognizable anywhere around the globe.

- **Practical**—Once you learn about this tool, you can use it immediately for self-awareness, self-development, and in interactions with others.

- **Accurate**—The DISC method has a high predictive accuracy.

To explain this behavioral tool more in depth, when people take the assessment survey, they receive a score across four behavior styles. The D, I, S, and C each represent an acronym for the four styles. We will learn about each of these in depth in the following four chapters. The words associated with the DISC are as follows:

- **D** = **Dominance**
- **I** = **Influence**
- **S** = **Steadiness**
- **C** = **Compliance**

The scores across each of the four styles range from 0 to 100. Any score above 50 represents a highly observable behavior. As an example, one of the words to describe a High "I" or influence style, is talkative or gregarious. So, if someone scores 50 and above on the "I" scale, they will likely be talkative and gregarious. The key thing to realize is that the higher the score, the more pronounced the behavior will be. Someone with a score of 95 will be much more talkative and gregarious than someone at 60. When you take the assessment, it will give you a score across all four of the styles.

Primary High DISC Behavior Style

The highest score is called the Primary High Style, or the most observable behavior and communication style of a person. Any other style above 50, which is not the Primary High Style, is called the Secondary High Style. The importance of Secondary High Styles takes precedence the further up it is from the 50. Someone may exhibit three styles above the 50 mark, which means they exhibit a bit of all three styles. However, the most predominant observable behavior is the one with the highest score. Again, the higher the score is from 50, the more pronounced the behavior and communication style is. Any score above the 50 mark is called "high."

As an example, if someone has the following DISC score:

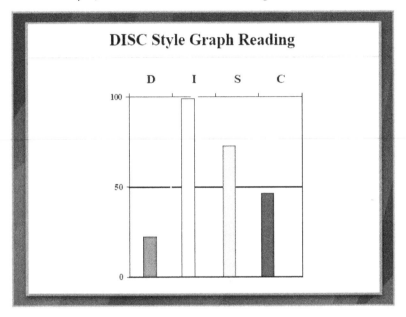

- **D = 20**
- **I = 100**
- **S = 70**
- **C = 47**

In this example, this person's Primary High Style is "I" because it represents the highest score and farthest above the 50. Then, the Secondary High Style is the "S" because it's also above 50. Simply put, as both are above the 50 mark, this person exhibits both High I and S behavior. However, the "I" takes precedence over the "S" because it is the higher score. Therefore, this person's Primary High Style is "I" because it is the highest and most observable to others who might interact with this person.

BOOK TERMINOLOGY

Speed of Adversity—The "speed of adversity" is referred to several times. Basically, it means adversity is hitting us faster and harder than ever, potentially leaving us less time to respond in a proactive, productive manner. A key to this book is that if you don't have the awareness and skills to recognize adversity, you may not be as effective at handling it as you need to be. Understanding your DISC style can assist you in understanding the intensity of your response to adversity.

Speed of Adversity and Intensity of Style

The Speed of Adversity topic has been discussed, and this could take more relevance on the intensity of someone's style. As stated, adversity is hitting us faster, leaving less time to respond productively. That may be a bigger factor if your primary DISC Style is stronger. As an example, a High D can be impatient and short-fused, with the emotional response of fight. If my score on the D is 100, versus someone whose score is 65, I may struggle with adversity a tad more because of the intensity of my style. In turn, fight mode at 100 is more difficult to recognize and control than fight mode at 65. I'm not saying this is true for all people in all situations. However, it is indeed something someone with a High D score should possibly consider and be on the look for.

Human Beings are Complex

Now, you may be thinking: people are not so easily categorized, are complex, and not solely one style. And you're correct. Typically, we are a blend of several of the four styles. I, as an example, am a Primary High S, with Secondary High D. So, when I consider my response to adversity of some sort, I must consider that blend. Just as I'm not solely D, I, S, or C, my potential emotional response to adversity is not solely freeze, fight, or flight. It can actually be more of a blend of freeze, first, then fight, second. You'll learn why in the subsequent chapters.

So, yes, we are complex, but typically, there is one style that manifests as most prevalent, and that is what is most observable when understanding ourselves and others. My Primary High S is what manifests and/or is most observable. But my high D must be considered, too.

The bottom line is that we all have different fingerprints and DNA unique to us. Doesn't it make sense that we each have different behavioral styles? So, once again, the key to that self-awareness is understanding our styles (primary and secondary) so we can understand our behavior during times of adversity. If we can understand that, we will better manage it when it happens.

Behavior and Communication 101: Back to the Basics

This tool is a foundational cornerstone for my business. I use it with my developmental coaching clients, which I will use to illustrate several examples in upcoming chapters, and in workshops. However, it's also helped me personally and professionally as well. This tool provides me with a powerful foundational element for understanding myself and other people. Any time where I've been successful in my life, I have had a clear understanding of that success' foundational element. Whether it was the foundational elements of reading, writing, and arithmetic; the 4 Ps of marketing (product/pricing/placement/promotion); or blocking and tackling in football, the DISC behavioral tool has provided me, my clients, friends, and others with an excellent tool for understanding themselves, and other people. It allows us to learn how to better communicate with others and how to deal with change, risk, conflict, failure, etc. Before I move forward, I want to make a few important points.

No Right or Wrong Behavior Style

Often these types of assessments gain a bad reputation because of the method by which they are administered and taught. As an example, they can be used to pigeonhole people. I have heard people say, *"Because you are a certain behavior or personality style, you could never be a manager, leader, or whatever."* This is NOT how I use this tool, nor is it how it should be used. Yes, the DISC behavioral tool will give indicators of how someone might do in a certain scenario or job function, but it isn't the be all and end all. Who am I to tell someone they cannot be a leader based on their DISC style? The tool only gives me insight into what I can do to help that person become an effective leader, which is how I use it. I stand by the opinion that anyone, of any style, can become effective if they can leverage their style successfully.

I will be reviewing the four styles in the next four chapters. To help you better understand them, you need to consider that we will be reviewing each from a one-style perspective. Meaning, we will consider the person is solely one of these styles alone, and no other. The purpose is to help you realize the unique and differentiating aspects of each. Always keep in mind that we are often a blend of more than one style.

FREE DISC Behavioral Survey—TTI Success Insights® Report

As an added benefit, you can take a shortened version of the DISC Survey and receive your personalized TTI Success Insights® report. This customized TTI Success Insights® report will contain four sections:

- Natural & Adapted Graphs

    - Natural Graph is your style when you are either totally stressed or totally relaxed. It's basically who you are "naturally." As a note, most of your report will consist of your "blended" Natural Style (meaning it will take into account all of your DISC style scores even though some aren't above the 50 mark). This is the more important and relevant graph for you now.

    - Adapted Graph is your style either in a new and unfamiliar environment OR what you think your workplace may require you to be.

- General Characteristics—A several paragraph narrative on your blended Natural Style score.

- Communication Tips—Tips for what and what not to do when communicating with people of the other four DISC Styles.

- Professional & Personal Development Pages—Areas where you can make a developmental plan of action based on your report and style.

* Please remember that this report is not necessarily saying it is 100% you. This report analyzes behavioral style; that is, a person's manner of doing things. Is the report 100% true? Yes, no, and maybe. This report is only measuring behavior. We only report statements from areas of behavior in which tendencies are shown. To improve accuracy, feel free to make notes or edit the report regarding any statement that may or may not apply, but only after checking with friends or colleagues to see if they agree.

Based on scientific research, the TTI Success Insights® report version of DISC has a very high predictive accuracy (this is the version I use in this book, and my consulting work). Use this report as a guideline and gauge into your behavior. Select verbiage that makes sense and leverage it for your growth and development. If you don't agree with something, then ask someone who knows you. If they agree it's you, then that could be a blind spot into how you view yourself, versus how others view you. If they agree a statement is not you, then disregard it and figure it's something that falls out of that high predictive accuracy.

DEVELOPMENTAL TOOLS

To take this *free* DISC survey and receive your personalized TTI Success Insights® Report, just visit www.gavatorta.com. Then click on the *In Defense of Adversity* book icon and visit the **IDOA Resources** section for the survey link. Once you complete the survey, your personalized report will be emailed directly to you (short page example below).

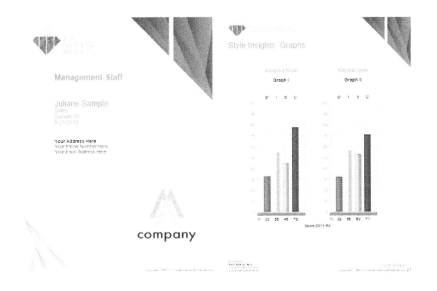

READER CALL TO ACTION

1. List 3-5 Key Takeaways/Learnings from Chapter 4.

2. Think of someone you have issues communicating/connecting with OR need to interact better with (write their name).

   - List 4-8 words that describe them (i.e. aggressive, gregarious, quiet, contemplative ... any words that come to mind).
     (Note: There is a graphic on the next page you can use for this exercise)

   - List whether this person is more Fast-Paced/Outgoing **OR** more Cautious/Reflective.

   - List whether this person is more People-Oriented **OR** more Task-Oriented.

   - List whether this person is more Direct **OR** Indirect.

* NOTE: We will revisit this information later in Chapter 10

IN DEFENSE OF ADVERSITY BEHAVIOR STYLE PROFILE TOOL

PERSONS NAME: _____

DESCRIPTORS:
(4-6 Words to describe this person)

_____

INDICATOR #1: _____
(Fast-Paced/Outgoing **OR**
Cautious/Reflective)

INDICATOR #2: _____
(Task **OR** People Oriented)

INDICATOR #3: _____
(Direct **OR** Indirect)

CHAPTER 5

HIGH D, DOMINANT STYLE

The dominant director, the driver, the D
Unconquerable, demanding, aggressive, free
Brave, decisive, competitive, tough
Up to the task, direct, sometimes rough!

Quick to the draw, flip with the lip
You'll get it direct, straight from the hip
They'll climb any mountain, nothing's too high
They aim to succeed, whatever they try.

Results is the focus, press on to new heights
Along the way, expect a few fights
Don't take it personal, they just speak their mind
So, pick up the pace, or get left behind.

You may smirk a little when you hear them rant
Of all that they'll win if their wish you grant
Give them a challenge that's brave and bold
Stand back and watch as they bring home the gold!
~

-Randy Widrick-[16]

Real-World High D

Tom was one of my fastest-paced clients. He was a high-level manager in the corporate world and a master at teaching his teams the basics of sales and marketing. The fundamentals he taught his team helped him become known as the top trainer and developer of talent in the company.

Tom was a forceful, aggressive, and challenging manager. He was direct and very fact-based. He didn't mince words and he carried himself well. He was outspoken and very talented. He loved change and taking risks. In addition, he never backed away from a fight, whether it was with internal marketing personnel or upper level management. He was guided by his confidence.

Tom was skilled at taking many data points to build a case for a sale. He had the unique ability to cut through all the analytics and summarize the findings into no less than five powerful points.

Tom had his strengths, but at times was known as a bull in a china shop. He had a colleague call him a rock-eater. Sometimes his directness got him in hot water, but for the most part, he was respected by his team and customers for his candor and no-nonsense approach.

I knew that to have my best results with Tom, I had to be prepared. When coaching and making recommendations to him, I had to have my facts straight and make my case in bullet-point fashion. He was a busy guy and for him, time was of the essence. The more buttoned-up and prepared I was, the more successful my times were when coaching him.

Tom was a typical High D, Dominant behavior style.

The Primary High D basic communication style is straightforward, no BS. You will definitely know where they are coming from, as they don't mince words.

THE HIGH D COMMUNICATION STYLE

To help you better understand the styles, we will review various attributes which include words and indicators to describe them, how they deal with change, risk, and conflict, as well as other interesting identifiers. Please keep in mind that as you review each of these four styles separately, the information pertaining to each of them assumes that this is the sole "Primary High Style" (i.e. there are no other scores above 50, except the one which we are discussing in the respective chapter).

Descriptors:

The 24 basic words, or as I call them, descriptors, to describe someone of the Dominant style are as follows:

1.	Direct	13.	Strength
2.	Daring	14.	Goal-oriented
3.	Forceful	15.	Problem solver
4.	Innovative	16.	Quick
5.	Blunt	17.	Challenge-oriented
6.	Decisive	18.	Persistent
7.	Competitive	19.	Demanding
8.	Strong-willed	20.	Impatient
9.	Bold	21.	Self-starter
10.	Results-oriented	22.	Adventurous
11.	Domineering	23.	Responsible
12.	Aggressive	24.	Strong ego

Indicators:

In addition to the descriptors, there are three measures across all four styles that can be used to understand each style better. These measures are called Indicators, and they are important in reading or profiling the styles of people we interact with. We will discuss this further in Chapter 10.

- The first indicator asks, is the style Fast-Paced/Outgoing OR Cautious/Reflective?

- The second indicator asks, is the style People-Oriented OR Task-Oriented?

- The third indicator asks, is the style Direct or Indirect?

So, from a High D perspective, on the first Indicator they are fast-paced/outgoing and more extroverted. Regarding the second Indicator, they are task-oriented, meaning they would rather work on a task than focus on people situations. It is not that they don't like people, but they are high energy "doers," so they like working on tasks that drive them to finish the work.

Lastly, regarding the third Indicator, they are very direct. You will not need to worry about not knowing where they stand on an issue, as High D's don't mince words.

Simply put, High D styles are gifted in getting tasks accomplished and are very motivated by authority and challenges. The more tasks and challenges you give them, the happier and more productive they will be.

Change, Risk, Conflict, and Decision Making:

Also important is the knowledge of how each of these styles deal with change, risk taking, and conflict. Knowing these facts is imperative in helping us understand how we may respond to unexpected change, the need to take a risk, or experiencing conflict with others. If you are talking about making a change with a person who doesn't like change, it is important to realize this so you can help them with the process. This means connecting.

High D styles love change and are bigtime risk takers. They're also willing to take the initiative during such times. Stagnation will totally bore the High D, so fast-paced, changing, high-risk environments are where they will flourish.

Regarding conflict, High D people are fighters; they won't back down easily. The interesting point is that they don't take a conflict personally, it is just how they respond.

Lastly, their decision making tends to be very fast and very decisive. Typically, they will make their decisions based on facts, evidence, and information. All of these are delivered in buttoned-up, straightforward form.

Some other helpful facts about the High D

Outstanding Characteristics

1. Need to Direct—They have an inherent need to direct and take

control of a situation. As I said above, they are basically extroverted people, so they will usually give their opinion in clear, specific language. If the group or discussion is moving a little slowly, expect them to step up to the plate and push the group along. Given the authority and responsibility, they can take you to new heights that might have previously been considered impossible.

2. Challenge—Always provide them with a challenge. If a job isn't challenge any more, expect them to flounder. They must have a continual problem to solve, a new challenge, or a mountain to climb. If there is no challenge, they will take the initiative and create one.

3. Desire to Win—They love to win and in their eyes, living is winning. They are driven to win in both the corporate world, as well as on the golf course. Vince Lombardi's famous quote, "Winning isn't everything, it's the only thing," is the perfect description of a High D approach to each situation, both personally and professionally.

4. Direct Communication—In dealing with people, a High D will be direct and to the point. No flowery words will be present as they say what they think. They may unintentionally come across as being too blunt to some people who are of other styles. They will take issue, possibly heatedly, if they disagree, but will seldom hold a grudge. As I said above, they will fight, but will not take it personally. After they have spoken their mind, they tend to forget about it—no harm, no foul.

Value to the Team

1. Bottom-Line Organizers—They are very results-oriented, so whenever they are given the authority, they will cut through all the needless steps to get the job done. Oftentimes, traditional paper-pushing activities in organizations add nothing to the value of the product turned out. Give the High D the job, set broad boundaries, and they will move mountains!

2. Self-Starters—Given a task, the responsibility, and authority, they will work long hours to show you that they can make it happen. Being that High D's are self-starters, there is no need to push them to get them going.

3. Forward-Looking—They focus on the possibilities of what can happen. They are fearless. Obstacles represent challenges to overcome, not a reason to stop. There is no need to worry, as you should expect

them to go for the gold.

4. Place High Value on Time—They are driven by efficiency; the quicker, the better. They are interested in how much can be accomplished in the least amount of time. They will speed up others and the process, but expect other styles to resist the change and fast pace.

5. Challenge-Oriented—Worrying about a challenge is not even an option they will consider. They must have a challenge to be motivated and thrive. If there is a challenge, they will take it on, regardless of how impossible, and they will focus all their energies on making it happen. If they are not challenged, they will create one.

6. Competitive—They love to win, and view winning as everything. Any competitive situation will motivate them to succeed and to perform better.

7. Initiate Activity—In sports terminology, they are the athlete saying, "Give me the ball; I'm going to win this game!" They are not ones to sit around, remain stagnant, and discuss options. They will take the bull by the horns and initiate activity to get desired results.

The Ideal Environment for them is one that is fast-paced and can constantly provide new challenges. Also important are

- Freedom from control, supervision, and details
- Evaluation based on results, not process or method
- An innovative and futuristic-oriented environment
- Non-routine work with challenges and opportunity
- A forum to express their ideas and viewpoints

Famous High Ds—Putting a Famous Face to the Name

In my interactions, I'd say that Barry Alvarez was very High D. He may have some secondary High I, but his dominant personality jumps out at you the very second you meet him. He's no-nonsense, direct, engaging, and commanding. When Barry enters the room, you immediately feel his presence. Some other High D's you may be more familiar with:

1)   Barbara Walters

2) Mark Cuban

3) Hillary Clinton

4) Kevin O'Leary of *Shark Tank*

5) Donald Trump

6) General Patton

7) Vince Lombardi

READER CALL TO ACTION

1. List 3-5 Key Takeaways/Learnings from Chapter 5.

2. Do you think you're a High D, and if so, why?
   (or if you took the survey, are you?)

3. List some people in your world who may be High D.

   - What makes you say that this is their style?

   - How do you tend to get along with them?

   - What potential issues might you have with them (if any)?

   - When was a time that things did go well with them, and why do you think it happened?

CHAPTER 6

HIGH I, INFLUENCER STYLE

Influencer, expressive, sanguine, the I
Life's full of hope, the limit's the sky
Enthusiastic, fun, trusting, charming
Confident, optimistic, popular, disarming.

Words smooth as cream as they talk to you
Winning you over to their point of view
A sparkling eye, a smile that's bright
In the dark of night, the I sees the light.

A person with a need to be liked
Inspiring the team to continue to fight
Talking a lot while getting work done
Don't worry a bit, work should be fun.

A joke or two, expect a high five
The High I adds humor, keeps things alive
Turn them loose and watch what's done
The team is inspired to work as ONE.
~

-Randy Widrick-[17]

Real-World High I

Laura was one of my favorite clients. She was an account manager who also led a sales team. She was excellent at diffusing difficult situations between the different factions of people that she interfaced with at work. Whether it was internal political strife or disagreements between her sales team and their customers, Laura was the calming force of reconciliation.

Laura was a very outgoing, friendly, and extroverted manager. She was always upbeat and saw the positive in any situation. She was a moderate risk taker and change didn't seem to faze her. Although she was good with difficult people, she would rather run than face a fight. She was a very personable and cheerful manager to her team.

Laura didn't dwell on facts, but gathered her energy from being around other people. She had a way of making the angriest customer cool down and become rational.

Along with these strengths came weaknesses. Because she was so people-oriented, she tended to trust people indiscriminately. In addition, she was guided by her image of what people thought of her. When times were good and her career was on the upswing, she felt great. However, when she was in situations where her image was tarnished, she responded negatively, and it hurt her greatly. This was often where we spent our time working together.

I had my best results with Laura when I appealed to her personality. I never worked with her without first chatting a bit about her personal life. She wanted me to be knowledgeable about every aspect of her life, personally and professionally. In addition, I appealed to her "image." When she did good things, I complimented her and celebrated her wins and successes; that approach greatly aided my work with her.

My client Laura exhibited typical High I, Influencer, behavior.

The communication style of a High I is very friendly and informal. They love being with and around others as they get their energy from people.

THE HIGH I COMMUNICATION STYLE

Descriptors

The 24 basic descriptors of someone of the High I style are as follows:

1. Enthusiastic	13. Emotional
2. Friendly	14. Poised
3. Trusting	15. Popular
4. Talkative	16. Charming
5. Stimulating	17. Confident
6. Gregarious	18. Generous
7. Persuasive	19. Good mixer
8. Optimistic	20. Effusive
9. Convincing	21. Inspiring
10. Influential	22. Spontaneous
11. Open-minded	23. Sociable
12. Affable	24. Personable

Indicators

Regarding the three Indicators, the High I style is, firstly, fast-paced/outgoing, very extroverted. There will be no evidence whatsoever of introversion. They will not only plan the party, they will host and be the focus of it, ensuring that everyone has a stellar time.

As expected on Indicator two, they are people-oriented, as opposed to task-oriented. They don't like working on tasks, as it bores them. They gain their steam and energy from people.

Lastly, on the third Indicator, because of their strong people orientation, they don't like being direct, especially in dealing with an issue that will hurt other people's feelings. This often poses problems for them, especially with people who like to be dealt with in a direct manner.

Because of their strength in dealing with people, High I's are very gifted in persuading others. In fact, they love persuading others to their point of view. As I mentioned with my client Laura, they are very motivated by their image, but this motivation can be a double-edged sword. If their image is positive, they will be motivated and happy. On the counter side, if their image is tarnished, it can be devastating.

Many of the High I clients I work with suffer from this dilemma. If, for some reason, a high level person in the organization is unhappy with them, doesn't like them, or has put a halt on their career advancement, it proves very difficult for them. I have run into this dynamic many times. I spend most of the coaching work helping them "re-brand" themselves in the organization to re-build their image and not be driven by what others think.

Change, Risk, Conflict, and Decision Making

Regarding change and risk-taking, High I's may not notice change because their emphasis is not on the event of change, but the people involved. If change involves people, they will be very engaged and concerned about the effects. If not, it may not resonate as much. They are moderate risktakers, depending on the situation. Remember, they are people-oriented. If the risk proves helpful to people, their willingness to take that risk will rise; however, if it might prove detrimental to people, that willingness will lower.

Being people-focused, they will run before getting into a confrontation. They are good at reconciling different factions, but that doesn't mean they will engage in a fight. So, if a serious conflict were to arise, they would avoid it.

Decision making will primarily be based on the strength of the relationship and rapport. High I's will be more willing to make a good decision if they like and trust someone. Don't overwhelm them with facts, data, or numbers, as it's about building rapport, them getting to know you, and you getting to know them.

Outstanding Characteristics

1. Need to Interact—Being people-oriented, they have an inherent need to interact, and love opportunities to verbalize and communicate. They have a tendency to talk smoothly, readily, and at length, using friendly contact and verbal persuasion as a way of promoting a team effort. They will consistently try to inspire you to see their point of view.

2. Need to Be Liked—Based on their concern for their image, they want to be liked and usually like others, sometimes indiscriminately. They get their energy from people, so they prefer not to be alone. They have a need for social affiliation and acceptance. They possess a high level of trust in others and, on the downside, may be taken advantage of by people. Based on the image concept, social rejection is a fear for them. The key to connecting with them is to praise in public and rebuke in private. This is true for most people, but especially for this style. They are incredibly optimistic, excel at building on the good in others, and see the positive side of a negative situation. You might say they see the world through rose-colored glasses.

3. Involvement—Being very energetic and active, they will be involved in just about everything. At their best, they promote trust and confidence, and feel they will persuade people to the kind of behavior they desire. They usually perform very well in situations where poise and smoothness are essential factors.

4. Emotional—Emotion is very difficult for them to contain. They do tend to wear their "heart on their sleeve," and their face is very expressive of the emotions they are experiencing. Their positive enthusiasm is very contagious, causing others to jump on whatever bandwagon the High I is on.

Value to the Team

1. Optimism and Enthusiasm—Since they have a strong people-orientation, they possess a great ability to motivate and get the team excited. When faced with adversity, the optimism and enthusiasm they exude will keep the team together.

2. Creative Problem Solving—They possess a very creative mind and, if allowed, will be ingenious in their ability to come up with new and creative ideas and solutions to problems.

3. Motivate Others Toward Goals—Leadership is the ability to move people toward a common goal. They excel at motivating people through positive interaction and persuasion. This ability causes others to want to work together as a team.

4. Positive Sense of Humor—Because of their gregarious attitude, they add fun to the team and the tasks at hand. Studies have proven

that productivity is increased as a team begins to have fun. High I's add that natural, fun, humorous element to the team.

5. Team Players—Since they need a lot of people interaction, they are very good team players. They love working together in teams because it means having fun while getting the job done.

6. Negotiate Conflict—Their strength with people means that they are natural mediators. Since they do not like conflict, they can verbally persuade both sides to come to an agreement. Part of this is due to their ability to focus on the bright side of the issues. Also, if both factions know the High I mediator, they both probably like him/her.

7. Verbalize Articulately—If there is a presentation to be made, an argument to be won, or someone who needs to be persuaded into something that is good for all, send in a High I. In these situations, they will paint an optimistic picture of the possibilities and have a greater chance of achieving the desired results, not to mention the fact that they will enjoy the opportunity to verbalize.

The Ideal Environment for them is one that is open, flexible, and fun. Also important are:

- Assignments with a high degree of people contact
- Tasks involving motivating groups and establishing a network of contacts
- Democratic supervisors with whom they can associate
- Freedom from control
- Multi-changing tasks

Famous High I's—Putting a Famous Face to the Name

Some examples of famous High I personalities are:

1) Bill Clinton

2) Steve Martin

3) Eddie Murphy

4) Lori Greiner of *Shark Tank*

5) Jim Carrey

6) Jay Leno

7) Shaquille O'Neal

(Note: Daymond John of *Shark Tank* would be a prime example of a blended High D, High I Style)

READER CALL TO ACTION

1. List 3-5 Key Takeaways/Learnings from Chapter 6.

2. Do you think you're a High I, and if so, why?
   (or if you took the survey, are you?)

3. List some people in your world who may be High I.

   - What makes you say that this is their style?

   - How do you tend to get along with them?

   - What potential issues might you have with them (if any)?

   - When was a time that things did go well with them, and why do you think it happened?

CHAPTER 7

HIGH S, STEADINESS STYLE

The steady relater, amiable, High S
Mild, laidback, patient, no stress
Stable, sincere, passive, serene
Great listening skills, an ace on the team.

Hard at work behind the scenes
Helping others to do what's best for the team
Others will tire, the S will finish
Determined to stay till the task has diminished.

Loyal, devoted, they'll be here for a while
Jumping around just isn't their style
Won't leave a job until it's over
Finish one first, you're not a rover.

Acutely aware of people's needs
Responding to personal hurts on the team
Although appearing slow in the jobs they do
When it comes to a team, the S is the glue.

~

-Randy Widrick-[18]

Real-World High S

Stephanie was my steadiest and warmest client. She was an easygoing manager with her staff. Her thought process was very methodical. She was what I would call a quiet leader.

In addition, she had the rare blend of understanding "the numbers," though she would always rather interface with people than work on a task.

Stephanie wasn't outgoing, but she had great rapport with people. On a one-on-one level, she was terrific. She was steady, relaxed, and non-emotional—so much so that her counterparts called her "Even Steven," an affectionate play on her name. She didn't like fast change, as she needed time to feel comfortable with it. Give her time to change and she was fine, but forcing something on her last minute was very frustrating. In addition, she was a moderately low risk taker.

Stephanie was excellent at solving problems with people and was fantastic in creating stable, peaceful work environments, despite pressure that might have been brewing.

Even with the stable environment, sometimes her downfall was not addressing issues head-on with certain employees and customers. At times, she tolerated conflict amongst staff. Her drive for peace and stability often clouded her judgment in adverse situations. In addition, her non-emotional approach was sometimes mistaken as being aloof to the situation.

I knew that to have my best results with her, my approach needed to be very steady and non-pushy. The best manner I could take was to provide an environment where she could come to her own conclusions. If I moved casually with her and presented my ideas in a patient manner, I would eventually win her over. It wasn't that she was not a fast learner, she just needed time to gain a lay of the land and then she'd be a master at anything she tried. She jokingly said that her life and career mirrored that of *The Tortoise and the Hare* fable. She might not be the first out of the box, but she'd eventually win the race. I totally agreed with her self-assessment.

Stephanie was a typical High S, Steadiness behavioral style.

The High S communication style is warm, open, and sincere. They like interfacing with people and are excellent in one-on-one situations.

THE HIGH S COMMUNICATION STYLE

Descriptors

The 24 basic words to describe someone of the High S style are as follows:

1. Methodical
2. Systematic
3. Reliable
4. Steady
5. Relaxed
6. Modest
7. Passive
8. Possessive
9. Amiable
10. Predictable
11. Understanding
12. Mild
13. Friendly
14. Serene
15. Good listener
16. Sincere
17. Non-demonstrative
18. Team-player
19. Patient
20. Stable
21. Inactive
22. Paced
23. Collaborative
24. Closure

Indicators

Regarding the first Indicator, High S's are cautious/reflective, more introverted. They are not necessarily shy, but they use their introversion to re-energize. Many High S styles re-energize by being alone. I, for one, am a High S. So, as an example, after a workshop or speaking engagement, I enjoy my alone time. It could be a jog along the water or in a park, or it could be a quiet dinner. The point is that High S styles get their energy back by doing something alone.

For the second Indicator, they would rather interface with people than work on a task. Though it sounds confusing that High S is introverted, yet people-oriented, their introversion is taken from the perspective of how they derive and re-ignite their energy.

Lastly, on the third Indicator, they are much more indirect than direct, mainly for the same reasons as a High I, as mentioned in Chapter 5.

As indicated by Stephanie's story, High S's are gifted in solving people problems. They are also motivated by peace and stability.

Change, Risk, Conflict, and Decision Making

Regarding change, they don't like it and need time to prepare for it. I don't like it initially myself, but once I can gain the lay of the land regarding the change, I am normally fine. They are also low risk takers and oftentimes don't tolerate conflict. When I am working with a High S style, I need to help them set boundaries when facing conflict or an aggressive type person. Setting boundaries helps them become better at dealing with the conflict and stopping difficult situations from becoming worse.

Regarding decision making, High S styles move slowly and don't like to be coerced. If coerced, they may shut down and/or show little emotion. With an S, take your time and approach in a collaborative manner. Provide a combination of some facts and information, along with suggestions and collaboration, and give them time to process afterward.

Outstanding Characteristics

1. Need to Serve—They have an inherent need to serve others and help people out in a pinch. They are not selfish and always lend a hand to get the job done. People of the other styles may serve for differing reasons, but the High S has a natural tendency to serve. In other words, serving and helping energizes them.

2. Loyalty—They are loyal and do not switch jobs very often, preferring to remain with one company as long as possible. They will also tend to stay in a relationship for a long time, be it business or personal, for reasons of security and harmony. With the goal of harmony, they will become adaptable to the situation, modifying their behavior in order to achieve a sense of stability. That is why, like Stephanie, many are called "Even Steven."

3. Patient and Relaxed—Because of their non-emotional approach, High S styles show a cool, relaxed face. They are not easily triggered or explosive in nature. Although they are very active emotionally, they do not show their emotion. As introverted people, they hide their problems

and do not wear their heart on their sleeve. They've been known to lead their teams to great heights, even while going through incredible personal struggles.

4. Closure—Getting closure on anything is essential for them, be it a personal or professional matter. In other words, they must be allowed to finish what they start. To start several jobs and leave them undone is stressful to them. In a task-oriented situation, they should be given few tasks and be allowed to complete them before moving on. Having to juggle many balls at once also proves stressful.

Value to the Team

1. Dependable Team Players—They are viewed as great team players because they are always willing to help out. They usually stay in a situation for a long time, as their loyalty has a stabilizing effect on them and others.

2. Working Hard for a Leader and Cause—If they believe in a leader and the cause, they will work extremely hard to make things happen (other styles will also work as hard, but for different reasons). They will be quick to assist others in areas they are familiar with.

3. Great Listeners—Listening skills are a natural behavior for them. Even when interrupted, they will stop, look you in the eye, and listen. Having a great listening ability makes them natural at helping people work through problems. This skillset, combined with their logical thinking, make them great assets to have on the team.

4. Patient and Empathetic—Combined with great listening skills, they are very patient. They make great efforts to really try to understand the situation that the other person is in. Sometimes they can become too adapting. They will usually give the other person the benefit of the doubt and may stay in a situation or relationship too long, hoping that it will get better.

5. Good at Reconciling, Calming, and Stabilizing Factions—They are driven by a desire for harmony and peace, so they can be a great asset in stabilizing a conflict. Again, their patience, listening ability, and logical approach can bring them back into harmony and focus.

6. Logical and Step-Wise Thinker—They are great assets to get involved in the planning process. Oftentimes, goals are set and the plans

to get there are not even thought out. They can bring lofty ideas back to the realm of the real world and point out gaps and flaws in the plan due to their logical thinking process.

7. Will Finish Tasks Started—Closure is of the utmost importance to them. They can, but do not enjoy, juggling a lot of balls. A task that is started must be finished. They will finish the first task and then move on to the next. Also, by utilizing the ability to organize effectively, they will take the initiative to develop a system to get the job done.

The Ideal Environment for them is one that is peaceful, stable, and marked by a helpful atmosphere. Also important are:

- Jobs where the standards and methods are established.
- Environments where longstanding relationships can be developed.
- Personal attention and recognition for tasks completed and well done.
- Stable and predictable environment.
- Environment that allows time for change.

Famous High S—Putting a famous face to the name

Here are some famous High S styles:

1) Laura Bush

2) Mr. Rogers

3) Dick Winters of the infamous Band of Brothers

4) Gandhi

5) Robert Herjavec of *Shark Tank*

6) Joe Torre

7) Derek Jeter

READER CALL TO ACTION

1. List 3-5 Key Takeaways/Learnings from Chapter 7.

2. Do you think you're a High S, and if so, why?
   (or if you took the survey, are you?)

3. List some people in your world who may be High S.

   - What makes you say that this is their style?

   - How do you tend to get along with them?

   - What potential issues might you have with them (if any)?

   - When was a time that things did go well with them, and why do you think it happened?

CHAPTER 8

HIGH C, COMPLIANT STYLE

Compliant, analytical, melancholic, the C
Methodical, courteous, complete accuracy
Restrained, diplomatic, mature, and precise
Accurate, systematic, those standards are nice.

Planning, and organization done to perfection
The smallest of detail is no exception
Consistently clear and objective thinking
Gives a team top-notch results without blinking.

And when it comes time to make a decision
You'd best have the facts to accomplish the mission
The C at your side with all the correct facts
Will ensure the return of your investment won't lack.

Go by the book, follow the rules
Procedures are written, use the right tools
Standards are crucial, both now and later
In God we trust, all others use data.

~

-Randy Widrick-[19]

Real-World High C

Kim was my most cerebral, analytical client. She was in a leadership role and was one of the most analytically astute leaders I've ever seen. She had the ability to find solutions to any situation by leveraging facts and figures at her disposal.

She was contemplative, conservative, and careful. She was excellent at analysis and using facts, figures, and numbers to find solutions for the clients. She was reserved, an introvert, and was always more comfortable working on tasks to find solutions to problems. She was a very low risk taker, concerned about the effects of change, and would always avoid a confrontation.

She had the ability to analyze large amounts of information from various data points and sources. Kim would then be able to compile this information to present a wonderful, coherent presentation to prove her points and secure the sale.

However, her greatest skill was also her greatest curse, as she often suffered from analysis paralysis. In addition, she was highly risk-averse, so getting her to act on recommendations was often like pulling teeth. This was also a source of frustration for her manager and interoffice personnel.

To get the best results with her, the main thing I focused on was making her comfortable with the changes I recommended and the risks I asked her to take. Minimizing the fear of the changes I recommended, and removing as much risk as I could, was key to Kim's development. Once I could provide the factual reasons for taking the initiative from my recommendations, she would be assertive; she did not respond to emotional pleas. As with all High C type people, you must remove risk and ensure they are comfortable with changes. If you cannot solve those two areas, it will be very difficult to get them to act quickly, if at all.

My client Kim was a typical High C, Compliant behavior style.

The communication style of a High C is very logical and detailed. They are not driven by emotion, strictly facts.

THE HIGH C COMMUNICATION STYLE

Descriptors

The 24 basic words to describe someone of the High C style are as follows:

1. Analytical	13. Logical
2. Contemplative	14. Conventional
3. Conservative	15. Courteous
4. Exacting	16. Mature
5. Careful	17. Diplomatic
6. Perfectionist	18. Patient
7. Accurate	19. Systematic
8. Conscientious	20. Cautious
9. Evasive	21. Specific
10. Fact-finder	22. Cerebral
11. Restrained	23. Detailed
12. Precise	24. Number-driven

Indicators

For the first Indicator, all High C people, like my client Kim, are cautious/reflective, more introverted. For the same reason, on the second Indicator, they are obviously more task-oriented than people-oriented. And lastly, on Indicator three, they are more direct versus indirect. They don't seek confrontation, but since they are risk-averse, they would rather be direct than be wrong or unsure of something. Again, the reason for this is tied to their risk aversion. Since they are fearful of mistakes and/or doing the wrong thing, they will be direct and let you know if they have a problem or question.

High C styles are gifted in analyzing tasks and procedures and are motivated by excellence and quality. They are typical dot the i's and cross the t's type of folks.

Change, Risk, Conflict, and Decision Making

Regarding change, they are concerned about the effects and, for similar reasons, are very risk-averse.

Although they are very direct, they will not seek conflict. In fact, they will do all they can to avoid it.

Lastly, regarding decision making, they are very slow and deliberative. Their decisions will be based on data, facts, and information, and will only be made once, to minimize or eliminate risk. They are not moved to make a decision because of a personal relationship, unless, of course, that relationship includes a trust on delivering facts and minimizing risk, allowing for slower decision making.

Outstanding Characteristics

1. Need for Procedures—They strive for a stable, orderly life, and tend to follow procedures in both their personal and business lives. Dependent upon procedures, they will usually stick to methods that have brought success in the past.

2. By the Book—The first and foremost rule of conduct for a Type C is to go by the book. They are very aware of, and sensitive, to the dangers of mistakes and errors, preferring a professional, disciplined approach to problem solving.

3. Perfectionists—They are constantly striving toward better ways of doing things. There is a right way to do things and a wrong way. They have a desire to be right, which usually means that they will come down on the safe side of a problem, where there is less risk.

4. Precise and Attentive to Detail—They are data gatherers and will collect all possible facts (maybe too many) related to a specific problem. They are systematic thinkers, precise, and attentive to detail. When called upon by other styles, they will tend to ask questions to clarify the data and go to the heart of the issue. They are very careful in thought and deed.

Value to the Team

1. Objective Thinkers– When dialoguing with them, the real world is the arena. They deal in the arena of objective fact and will make you prove your case. They bring a reality to planning, analyzing, and testing

the data for accuracy.

2. Conscientious—They take their work personally, almost as an extension of their being. The finished task is a reflection of their attention to small details. They are usually very loyal and will go the extra mile to get the job done.

3. Maintain High Standards—In a book called *The Wisdom of Team*, one characteristic was found on all high-performance work teams' commitment to the highest standards. High C's will even assist in writing the standards. With a quality focus, the High C assists the team in consistency of standards and operation, adding order to the scenario.

4. Define, Clarify, and Test—Great objective thinkers, High Cs will blow holes into plans that are not well-thought-out. Their skeptical nature looks at all possibilities before buying into a plan. Utilized in this way, they can be a great asset to any team. And don't argue with them unless you have your ducks in a row. Being aggressive collectors of data and information, they are walking computers, always analyzing, testing, and clarifying.

5. Ask the Right Questions—One of the most significant contributions the High C makes to any organization is asking the tough questions. This talent often leads to the changing of a shallow plan.

6. Diplomatic—If given the opportunity, High C's will be very diplomatic in sharing the data to support their conclusions. They prefer discussions void of emotional appeal.

7. Pay Attention to Detail—Many projects would be a total disaster if it weren't for the High Cs attention to detail.

The Ideal Environment for them is doing things right. Also important are:

- Places where critical thinking is needed and rewarded.

- Assignments that can be followed through to completion.

- Noise and people kept at a minimum.

- Close relationships with a small group of people.

- Environments where quality, and/or standards, are important.

Famous High Cs—Putting a Famous Face to the Style

Some famous High C's are:

1) Al Gore

2) Diane Sawyer

3) Sherlock Holmes

4) Mr. Spock of *Star Trek*

5) Alan Greenspan

6) Barbara Corcoran of *Shark Tank*

7) Kevin Harrington of *Shark Tank*

DEVELOPMENTAL TOOLS
Have you determined your DISC Style yet? Why not actually find out your DISC Behavioral Style now? To take this *free* survey, receive your personalized TTI Success Insights® Report, just visit www.gavatorta.com. Then click on the *In Defense of Adversity* book icon and visit the **IDOA Resources** section for the survey link. Once you complete the survey, your personalized report will be emailed directly to you.

READER CALL TO ACTION

1. List 3-5 Key Takeaways/Learnings from Chapter 8.

2. Do you think you're a High C, and if so, why?
(or if you took the survey, are you?)

3. List some people in your world who may be High C.

- What makes you say that this is their style?

- How do you tend to get along with them?

- What potential issues might you have with them (if any)?

- When was a time that things did go well with them, and why do you think it happened?

CHAPTER 9

EMOTIONAL TRIGGERS AND REPONSES

If your emotional abilities aren't in hand, if you don't have self-awareness, if you are not able to manage your distressing emotions, if you can't have empathy and effective relationships, then no matter how smart you are, you are not going to get very far.

~

-Daniel Goleman-

From Self-Knowledge to Self-Awareness

Now that you have a good understanding of the four DISC Behavioral Styles (as well as your DISC Style), the key is to use this knowledge to successfully face and overcome adversity. Hopefully with this review you did indeed gain deeper self-knowledge about your style and yourself.

The next step is building high self-awareness. The more we can understand what might trigger an emotional response, both from a DISC style and situational perspective, the more we can apply an appropriate response and work from a rational, reasoned approach, rather than an emotional one. In realizing that we have options or can develop new ones, we can thus proactively and productively address situations better in the future.

Essentially, the more we can learn about ourselves and what triggers our emotional responses, the more effective we can be at handling adversity and possibly leveraging options in our favor. Self-knowledge and self-awareness are vital. If we are not self-aware, we will not be nearly as productive in life. Having High Emotional Intelligence (EQ) is key as well.

What is Emotional Intelligence (EQ)

In an email, Jennifer Shirkani, speaker, expert on Emotional Intelligence (EQ), and author of the highly successful books *Ego vs EQ* and *Choose Resilience,* stated that:

> *"EQ is a set of skills that include one's ability to **recognize** their own impulses and moods; they can **read** situations accurately and **respond** most appropriately, depending on the situation or person they are dealing with. EQ is the demonstration of sensibility. Someone with high EQ can communicate with others effectively, can manage change well, is a good problem solver, uses humor to build rapport, has empathy, and remains optimistic even in the face of difficulty. These people can emotionally and mentally plug into others and can read the situation at hand and behave accordingly to get the best results for everyone."* [20]

How many stories do you hear about super high IQ people who have zero people skills or self-awareness? How many of you know these types of people? They may be brilliant, but have issues functioning themselves and with others. They can be easily angered, show impatience, be awkward with people, or are simply oblivious to others' needs. These people may be advanced intellectually, but struggle personally and emotionally in managing themselves and in dealing with others. Most often these people either have, or create, unnecessary difficulties for themselves and those people with whom they interact. These people may lack High EQ. So, the chances are, if you do not have a high EQ, you may have issues responding appropriately and productively in certain interactions with self and others.

In an article written in *Harvard Business Review* called "What Makes a Leader," EQ guru Daniel Goleman states:

> *"In my work, I discuss the amygdala being the emotional center of the brain. It is what detects threat and triggers the limbic system to go into fight or flight. For this reason, the amygdala has a hotwire to our reactions, bypassing the pre-frontal cortex ("thinking") part of the brain temporarily. As a practical matter, the amygdala serves a vital purpose for our survival, but it is also easily triggered and a bad judge—it interprets symbolic threats the same as physical*

ones. So, it takes the act of someone challenging you in a meeting at work the same as it would if a car was coming at you in a crosswalk. The goal with the amygdala is twofold: increase your self-awareness to know your triggers so you can predict what or who could trigger a response in you, and desensitize the amygdala by role playing or visualizing threatening situations so you can pre-plan a response before you get triggered." [21]

Goleman's quote ties directly back to Eric Parker's approach discussed in Chapter 4 for understanding the limbic system and cortex. The more astute we are at understanding and recognizing our emotional triggers, the more we will be able to manage our responses in a productive, rational, and reasoned manner.

The Non-Perceptive Leader—Low EQ in Action

As an example, one of my clients was a high-level director and leader in his company. He was very accomplished. However, his low self-awareness created many obstacles in his life. He was brilliant but had very low EQ. Several instances involved his behavior in department meetings. If he was in disagreement with something, he didn't merely argue his point, he would sigh, laugh out loud, or roll his eyes. This lack of self-awareness hurt him with his colleagues as they thought his outbursts were unwarranted and disrespectful. This created self-inflicted issues with his colleagues, which created greater problems, as they didn't take his insights seriously—most of them shut down and didn't communicate with him unless absolutely necessary.

Here was this brilliant man who diminished his leverage and reputation because he was so unaware of how his outbursts were perceived by others. Despite being accomplished and highly intelligent, he had very low EQ and it hurt him badly. He created unneeded adversity in his life. This added to his issue of dealing with adversity in general. It often overwhelmed him and his problems multiplied.

This is an example how someone with low EQ, caused by low self-awareness, ultimately created much adversity for himself and others. In this instance, disagreement was the emotional trigger for him, and fighting back with outbursts and being argumentative was the emotional response (aka fight). If this leader had had High EQ (strong self-awareness) he wouldn't have had these outbursts that were so noticeable to others. He'd have been aware of how his behavior could affect others, and in turn, could have responded rationally. His irrational behavior led to unnecessary trouble for him. It hurt him in his career, and with his colleagues, both of which carried over into his personal life as well. This was a large topic of our work together.

DISC and EQ

I'm certified in EQ as well, but the focus of this book is not EQ. However, I thought it important to discuss EQ in relation to being able to effectively deal with adversity.

I use the DISC Behavioral assessment tool to enable my clients to better improve their EQ. If you can become more aware of your DISC Behavioral Style, you can develop your EQ as well. This awareness will enhance your life and your interactions with others.

Connecting the Dots

So, let's revisit the four DISC styles from the vantage point of identifying what I call emotional triggers and emotional responses to adversity. As a reminder, DISC is not always directly black or white. This information is about self-knowledge, but also self-reflection—connecting the dots between your DISC style and historical responses to adverse situations. In other words, this is highly directional, but not perfect. It's all meant to make you think about yourself and gain more self-knowledge and self-awareness.

About Emotional Triggers

In this book, the definition of an "emotional trigger" is an adverse event or situation that may set up an unwanted emotional response. In other words, if we're not self-aware, conflict may send us into that limbic system emotional state of freeze, flight, fight. An emotional trigger can be an event, and/or other people, or a combination of both. So, an event-driven emotional trigger could include things such as change, the need to make a quick decision, loss of a job, a promotion, or an unexpected unfortunate event.

A person-based emotional trigger could be a person and/or an interaction with someone who drives you to that emotional state, such as a friend, spouse, colleague, or someone you have difficulties dealing with in general. Think of my low EQ client who I referenced a few paragraphs ago. He was emotionally triggered by colleagues, as he, in turn, triggered many of them as well.

BOOK TERMINOLOGY
Emotional Triggers—An emotional trigger is an adverse event, and/or person that may set up an undesired emotional response of freeze/fight/flight, or some combination of the three.

Sports Psychology Connection

In many instances people use this knowledge to their advantage—not saying you should necessarily do it. Have you ever heard the phrase "psyching someone out" or "getting in someone's head?" These are examples where an athlete may try to intimidate another by saying derogatory things or behaving in certain ways towards an opponent in an effort to frustrate them. Current UFC phenom Conor McGregor is a master at this. Muhammad Ali was too. They would incessantly verbally taunt their opponents, wearing them down mentally. Eric Parker said he used various techniques at times, most often subtle, to throw his opponent off prior to a kickboxing match. Essentially these people are triggering their opponents in an attempt to initiate emotional responses and get them in that limbic state of mind of freeze, fight, or flight.

The key if you are on the receiving end is to realize the game they're playing and not be drawn into it. Stay rational, stick to your plan, and remain in that cortex part of the brain.

About Emotional Responses

Your emotional response, as defined in Chapter 3, would be how you react to the emotional trigger, whether rationally, thoughtfully, or in the highly emotional limbic state. Is your response freeze, flight, fight, and/or some blended combination? Based on your trigger and DISC style, you can become aware when an undesired or adverse event happens and self-manage by ensuring you **prevent** the transfer of authority from the rational cortex-based response to the limbic system response. So, when an adverse emotional trigger hits, you will have a specific rational, reasoned, well-thought-out response, or responses.

Putting It into Action

Listed below are four real-world examples of coaching clients of mine, demonstrating how emotional triggers and responses manifested in their respective situations. These four examples illustrate a scenario, the emotional triggers, and responses of each DISC Behavioral style.

The High D—Emotional Triggers & Responses

Tim is a team sales leader of a consumer-packaged goods company who's conducting a substantial change initiative. As part of the change initiative, Tim delegates responsibility to various team members to help him drive the change rapidly. However, many of the team members seem hesitant and are dragging their feet. They don't seem to have bought into the change, and in turn are slowing the speed at which Tim wants this shift to occur.

Because of the slow pace, Tim loses his patience and is quite harsh with several of his team leaders. In addition to reprimanding them, he takes control of the situation himself, stops delegating, and drives the change initiative himself. After three months, the desired change and sense of urgency haven't improved, further driving Tim's anger and his team's frustrations. Morale plummets.

- **High D Emotional Triggers**—Some examples include losing, not enough change and/or not at a fast enough pace, wasting time, not being challenged or having growth opportunities, losing control.

- **High D Emotional Responses**—Some examples include anger, impatience, seeking control, moving too fast, taking too many risks, being stubborn, overstepping authority, being too direct, being argumentative, not listening well, being a one-way communicator, pushing rather than leading, lacking tact or diplomacy, and seeking a fight.

  - **High D Emotion**—The emotion of a High D is anger. A High D will tend to be quick to anger and have a short fuse. The higher and more pronounced the person's D Style, the shorter the fuse. By observing the intensity of the D's anger, the D factor can be quickly assessed as high or low when interacting with someone.[22]

- **Likely emotional response** = Fight.

High D—Emotional Repercussions

Tim's situation is common with High D's. High D's can get impatient, become argumentative, and take total control. This may make them feel better at the time but can be quite harmful in the long run. In this instance, although Tim thought his taking control would resolve the situation, it hindered it, harmed the team, and hurt morale. Tim's impatience cost him in the long run.

As a High D, if Tim was more aware of his trigger points such as, in this instance, change initiative, and the time it might take time to cultivate with some of his team, he would have been more aware of his responses of anger and impatience. He then could have managed this situation more productively.

High I—Triggers & Responses

Carrie works as a high-level customer service manager in a technology company. Due to some company issues, she and her team have been inundated with complaints both from internal and external customers. Due to these complaints, she's been asked to analyze data behind the complaints and supply a detailed report. She's catching a lot of heat and there have been grumbles about her performance, particularly wondering if she is in over her head. Prior to this situation, she was a stellar performer, even receiving numerous awards. However, this situation has shaken her self-confidence.

Since this occurred, she has become very distressed and discouraged. She either doesn't address personnel issues head-on, or most often glosses over issues with unrealistically optimistic expectations. Sometimes, she is even accused of not dealing with the real world and seeing things through rose-colored glasses. She is trying to uphold an upbeat, sunny attitude, but it is irritating many colleagues and team members. Once the "golden child" of the department, this whole dynamic has drained her of energy and made her doubt her own abilities.

- **High I Emotional Triggers**—Some examples include bad or harmed image, not enough freedom, not enough people interaction, too much data and information to analyze.

- **High I Emotional Responses**—Some examples include acting impulsively, inattentive to detail, difficulty planning and/or controlling time, overestimating ability to motivate others or change behavior, under-instructing and over-delegating, disconnecting, being unrealistic, overselling ideas, not facing issues, running away, avoiding confrontation, and seeing the world through rose-colored glasses.

  - **High I Emotion**—High I's believe the impossible can be done and will hold incredible optimism for the future. This optimism may not be totally grounded in data, facts, or reality.[23]

  - **Likely Emotional Response** = Flight.

High I—Emotional Repercussions

Carrie's response to this situation is not unique. So many times, I've have to work with High I's whose image has been tarnished and it's devastating to them. This, in turn, can negatively affect others, in this instance, her colleagues, team, and most importantly, customers. In addition, High I's are not as astute in, or motivated by, analyzing data and information. When they are forced to do so, it can be difficult for them.

If Carrie was more aware of her trigger points, such as angry customers, the need to successfully analyze data, and her image as top performer taking a hit, she could have predicted the response. In this case, her rose-colored glasses approach was a form of "flight" emotional reaction.

High S—Triggers & Responses

Beth has quite a busy schedule as a college professor, teaching her class and dealing with students and administration. A recent directive has come down requiring her to handle several projects with short deadlines. Although her boss, the dean, has praised her skills, Beth becomes frustrated, as these projects have thrown off her well-planned schedule and classroom goals.

Beth is frustrated primarily because she has so much on her plate already, and she can't muster the courage to tell the dean that she has too much to do already. When the dean asks if she's okay with it, she shuts down and murmurs, "Sure, no problem." In addition, she is also frustrated, as she desires to work with some of her colleagues on this project, but all seem to be working on their own. She's grown stressed and highly unmotivated.

- **High S Emotional Triggers**—Some examples include too much change, risk, too many tasks at hand with no closure, forced to make decisions on short notice, being overwhelmed, lack of collaboration from others, no time to think things through.

- **High S Emotional Responses**—Some examples include taking criticism as a personal affront, resisting change for the sake of change, difficulty establishing priorities, internalizing feelings, waiting for others to act first, projecting a false sense of compliance, being too hard on themselves, staying involved in a situation too long, no sense of urgency, shutting down, not communicating, tolerating difficult situations, and showing no emotion.

  - **High S Emotion**—High S's can be emotional. However, they have an inherent ability to mask their emotions. This is great if they're playing poker, but not so good if they're internalizing situations, not expressing their opinions, and suppressing their emotions.[24]

  - **Likely Emotional Response** = Freeze.

High S—Emotional Repercussions

Being a primary High S myself, I can attest to Beth's response to her dean's project requests. High S's aren't necessarily the best at getting thrown last-minute projects, especially when there is so much more already on the plate to address. In addition, not having collaboration in the department plays another factor in Beth feeling overwhelmed and somewhat demoralized.

If Beth was more aware of her trigger points of being overwhelmed when given-last minute projects, she would have predicted shutting down as the emotional response. The emotional response for the High S is non-emotion, or to shut down—in limbic terms, freeze.

High C—Triggers and Responses

Carl is a buyer at a large retailer. He is renegotiating a contract with two of his key vendors. The contract timing is rapidly coming to an end, and he needs proposals from both. Unfortunately, both have provided proposals with little and/or inaccurate data, making it difficult for Carl to come to a well-informed decision. This has caused issues for him, as he will not decide until he has all pertinent data.

With the deadline hitting and the lack of data, he is both angry and concerned. He's becoming less willing to make needed changes or take a risk with so little time and so little data. He is also getting pressure from his manager about the deadline, further driving Carl into his indecisive ways. Analysis paralysis is becoming stronger and his risk aversion is stressful.

- **High C Emotional Triggers**—Some examples include errors, mistakes, being pressed to make decisions quickly, too many interpersonal interactions.

- **High C Emotional Reponses**—Some examples include hesitating to act without precedent, being too critical, being bogged down in detail, internalizing feelings, being defensive, yielding to controversy, seeking solace with like-minded people, being too hard on selves, telling ideas as opposed to selling them, shutting down, overanalyzing, becoming too paralyzed to decide and/or act, and avoiding of conflict.

  - **High C Emotion**—The emotion of a High C is fear. The more pronounced the person's C, the more the individual will prefer low-risk decisions, following procedures, and going by the book.[25]

  - **Likely Emotional Response** = Freeze, possibly Fight

High C—Emotional Repercussions

As a High C, not having accurate information while being pressed to make a decision is incredibly trying. High C's are meticulous, data driven, and slow to make decisions. This situation has created incredible stress for Carl, and is causing even more analysis paralysis, which is not good when a deadline is rapidly approaching.

If Carl was more aware of his trigger points, such as deadlines and data to review, all in short order, he could have predicted his emotional response—a blended combination, in this instance, of both freeze and fight.

It's Not Black or White

As mentioned several times, a majority of us are not solely one style; we are blends of the various DISC Styles. There are many exceptions where people are solely High D, High I, High S, or High C, but it is by far not the rule. So, the way a High D, High I blended style may respond is different than a solely High D. The sole High D may just fight, whereas the High D, I blend may exhibit both Fight/Flight dynamics. It sounds counterintuitive, but people and behaviors can be complex. Strong self-awareness can help remove some of the complexity.

In addition, our behavioral styles can change through the years, depending on circumstances. So, concurrently, what triggers us may change, depending on those circumstances. This, in turn, drives our respective response. Once again, self-knowledge and self-awareness are key.

Considering DISC Style Blends

Now, I'll use myself as an example of how blended DISC styles can recognize their triggers and emotional responses. I'm a Primary High S, with secondary High D—both DISC scores close together, hovering in the 60s. My blended style plays out perfectly with both my triggers and responses. If I'm operating in the emotional limbic state, a big trigger is disturbing peace and stability by forcing me to make a quick decision. Remember, High S's are motivated by peace and stability and don't like to be pressed to decide anything quickly. Hence, I will shut down. I will show little emotion and start internalizing. This is very frustrating.

Then, being that I am High D, I may tend to feel angry about it. How hard I'm pressed to make the quick decision and give an answer will determine if I lose patience. My previous non-emotion now transitions into an emotional outburst, surprising most people since my initial response is usually shutting down. People may have thought I was okay because I showed little emotion and/or didn't speak my mind, but in truth, I was seething at being pressed and having my plan ruined. Often, this gets people thinking "Who peed in Steve's Wheaties today?"

Awareness of my blended style has helped me greatly in recognizing my emotional triggers so I can manage my responses accordingly. As an example, when my peace is disturbed and I'm forced to act, rather than initially shutting down, I attempt to deal with it directly by discussing realistic time frames and sharing my concern. I choose to seek options, having learned from past situations. Am I perfect? No. Sometimes I slip, but I'm better more often than not and am always seeking to learn from the situation rather than letting it control me. Essentially, by raising self-knowledge about my DISC style and self-awareness of my responses to adversity, I've also been able to raise my EQ. This knowledge and skill with the DISC tool can do the same for you.

Coaching Resolution

In these four instances in this chapter, my clients were responding to their situations emotionally, not rationally. Hence, our coaching work focused around using their DISC styles to raise awareness of their respective triggers/responses and then building a foundation of steps to help them better identify the triggers when adversity hit so they could apply the appropriate response and plan of action. In other words, help them better recognize how adversity played out in their lives, and then coach them to create, or recognize options. They didn't need to fall back on their typical emotional responses. We created new pathways for success. You'll learn more about this approach in upcoming chapters.

Next Steps

Oftentimes, our issues involve others, just as in the case with my client who had low EQ. Many of his issues revolved around interactions with his colleagues. With his uncontrolled outbursts, he provided unnecessary adversity for his colleagues. His behavior created problems for them, especially some who were sensitive to his outbursts. Since so many issues in our lives involve others, we need help in this arena as well. Fortunately, DISC is the perfect tool in this area as well.

The first obvious benefit of DISC is self-knowledge and self-awareness. It also can help people learn to communicate, engage, and interact with each other. In the next chapter, I will introduce some approaches that use the DISC tool to enable you to build trust, improve relationships, and minimize issues with others.

READER CALL TO ACTION

1. List 3-5 Key Takeaways/Learnings from Chapter 9.

    *   Based on your DISC Behavioral Style and your own personal experience, list situations that Trigger an Emotional Response from you (in other words what things, events, people may set of a Limbic System Response of Freeze/Fight/Flight?)

    *   When the Emotional Trigger occurs, how does it manifest (i.e. Freeze/Fight/Flight and/or some blend of the three)?

    *   What can you do to better deal with the Emotional Triggers when they occur?

    *   What can you do to better ensure a rational, reasoned response versus an emotional response?

CHAPTER 10

SUCCESSFULLY INTERACTING WITH OTHERS

To effectively communicate, we must realize that we are all different in the way we perceive the world and use this understanding as a guide to our communication with others.

~

-Anthony Robbins-

Adversity with Others

I think most would agree that many of our issues and difficulties, either realistic or perceived, are generated in interpersonal scenarios both personally and professionally.

Now that we've raised our self-awareness about our style, the key is being able to read and adapt to others. The foundation of that, once again, is based on DISC. The premise is this: if I know my style and can read others, I can adapt my approach to maximize results in my interactions. In other words, you'll be able to avoid unneeded situations and confrontations, or not let them escalate into something worse.

By learning about four basic DISC styles, you now have some tools to empower your decision making in dealing with others. Next, you need to learn to read the styles of others, and leverage your own knowledge of yours, for the purposes of effective communication and mutually rewarding relationships.

Style Differences

The key reason many of us have issues with others is that we are indeed different people and see the world through our unique backgrounds and experiences. Our DISC styles may be quite different as well. We behave, communicate, and are motivated differently. We deal with change, risk, conflict, and decision making differently. Let me give you a few examples of how easily a disconnect can manifest, just based on different behavior/communication styles.

Scenario #1: A sales rep, Kim, is calling on a customer, Dan. Their DISC behavioral attributes are listed below:

- Customer—Dan is no-nonsense, direct, straightforward, aggressive, a multi-tasker, and a very fact-based individual. He doesn't have time for idle chitchat.

- Sales Rep—Kim is gabby, emotional, loves chatting with people, and is extroverted. She's determined to win people over with her charm and personality.

- Based on these characteristics, what is Dan's DISC Behavioral Style? Kim's?

- Based on their style differences, what problems might exist, creating a disconnect?

Scenario #2: A personal relationship, where the DISC Behavioral Styles are listed below:

- Boyfriend—Rick is analytical, risk-averse, and quiet. His decision-making process is slow and he's more introverted.

- Girlfriend—Carla is direct, aggressive, and likes to control her destiny and the destinies of others. She is very competitive.

- Based on these characteristics, what is Rick's DISC Behavioral Style? Carla's?

- Based on their style differences, what problems might exist, creating a disconnect?

Scenario #3: A work environment situation between manager and subordinate

- Manager—Laura is friendly, introverted, methodical, team-oriented, and relaxed.

- Subordinate—Chris is risk-averse, aloof, analytical, direct, and careful.

- Based on these characteristics, what is Laura's DISC Behavioral Style? Chris'?

- Based on their style differences, what problems might exist to create a disconnect?

Style Clashes = Adversity

In the three scenarios, it is simple to see how and where disconnects in communication might occur. Because the styles are different, there is a chance for a disconnect and potential for serious issues. These issues lead to adverse situations for both parties:

- In Scenario #1—Buyer Dan is a High D style; Kim the sales rep is a High I style. Their potential clashes and issues may occur due to Kim being overly personal, talkative, and not as organized as Dan would like. In the role of customer, Dan could get frustrated by the lack of directness and facts with Kim's approach. This problem could lead to Dan (Fight) lashing out at Kim, and her not dealing with the situation productively (Freeze/Flight)

- In Scenario #2—Boyfriend Rick is a High C style; girlfriend Carla is a High D style. They both may become very frustrated with each other as Carla's aggressive approach may overwhelm Rick. Carla may get frustrated with Rick's slow-paced, slow decision-making style. This problem could lead to Rick shutting down (Freeze), which would further anger Carla (Fight).

- In Scenario #3—Manager Laura is a High S style; Chris is a High C. Laura may struggle with Chris not being as personal and collaborative as she'd like. In turn, Chris may not want to participate as part of the team, doing more projects on his own instead. In this instance, Laura could get frustrated and shut down (Freeze), and Chris might do the same.

In all these instances, each person is not necessarily wrong in their approach. In each style scenario, both people have strengths and potential weaknesses. The point of this exercise is to illustrate that many of our issues with others that cause difficulties are most often due to style clashes. The key to overcoming such clashes is, once again, raising self-awareness of styles, potential differences, and working to solve, or minimize, such scenarios. This chapter focuses on just that approach.

Step #1—Reading the Behavior Styles of Others

The key to improving interaction and avoiding unneeded issues with others is to first be able to clearly identify the DISC Behavior style in yourself and others. The key question is how, then, can you recognize and identify the DISC styles in others? Remember, most people are blends of various styles. However, there is almost always a most prevalent style to observe. That is what you're aiming for when you profile the DISC style of others. So I teach people to identify the most observable style when interacting with someone so they can then adapt accordingly.

Cues for Reading the 4 DISC Styles of others

In a majority of my workshops, I train my clients to "read" the DISC Behavioral Style of others using a simple process of Descriptors and Indicators (my clients will write these Descriptors/Indicators for another person):

- **Descriptors**—These are words that essentially describe each of the DISC Behavioral Styles. Match the words that best describe the person you're interacting with and where they best fall.

- **Indicators**—Out of the three Indicators below, identify which applies to this person as well:

    - Indicator #1—Is this person more Fast-Paced/Outgoing or more Cautious/Reflective?

    - Indicator #2—Is this person more People-Oriented or more Task-Oriented?

    - Indicator #3—Is this person more Direct or Indirect?

Based on what is captured/written, my clients simply match up how the Descriptors, and Indicators for this person best align with the respective attributes associated with each of the 4 DISC styles in the following graphic (you actually already captured this information for someone in the Reader Call to Action exercise at the end of Chapter 4).

Reading the 4-DISC Styles: Descriptors & Indicators			
DISC Style	D = DOMINANCE	I = INFLUENCE	S = STEADINESS	C - COMPLIANCE
High Descriptors	Ambitious	Expressive	Methodical	Analytical
	Forceful	Enthusiastic	Systematic	Contemplative
	Direct	Friendly	Reliable	Conservative
	Decisive	Demonstrative	Steady	Exacting
	Independent	Talkative	Relaxed	Careful
	Challenging	Stimulating	Modest	Deliberative
Indicator #1	Fast-Paced/Outgoing	Fast-Paced/Outgoing	Cautious/Reflective	Cautious/Reflective
Indicator #2	Task-Oriented	People-Oriented	People-Oriented	Task-Oriented
Indicator #3	Direct	Indirect	Indirect	Direct

The above information can give you insights into a person's respective DISC Behavioral Style. Is it a perfect art? No. Remember, people may not be solely one style. However, this step of reading "descriptors and indicators" will at least get you in the ballpark regarding someone else's style.

Step #2 - Adapting to the Styles of Others

These are good clues for you to recognize the styles of others. Now the key is, what do you do to minimize issues and improve interactions? That's where we'll go next. As you read these, also think about your style. Remember that you may need someone to approach you in the manner as your style. I'm a high S style. So, as I review the approaches for a High S, it helps me to understand my needs as well. I need to communicate that to others so they can best communicate and interact with me. In other words, I'm educating someone on my style and needs so we can successfully interact and, most importantly, avoid unnecessary conflict.

Adapting communication is not just a one-way street. You are not the only one that needs to adapt and adjust styles. As you build trust, it's perfectly all right to communicate your needs to others. It's much better to take that approach than sit back and be angry, cause issues, or even worse, let a situation fester until it blows up. The more we raise self-awareness in ourselves and understand others, the more robust our relationships will become.

We're Not the Same and That's Okay

One of the greatest football coaches ever was Vince Lombardi. Lombardi was known as a great leader, communicator, and motivator. One of the primary reasons he was good at all three is that he knew all his players were not built alike. He stated:

"You can't coach without criticizing, and it's essential to understand how to criticize each man individually. For instance, some can take constructive criticism in front of a group, and some can't. Some can take it privately, but some can only take it indirectly. Football is a motivation business, and on my team, I put on most of the motivation. The point is that I've got to learn forty ways to motivate forty men." [26]

This is one of my favorite quotes of all time, and I use it in nearly every workshop I conduct. I like it not solely because this was a quote by one of the most beloved, successful professional coaches of all time, but because it's this approach that made him so successful.

The key to Lombardi's success was the realization that not all his players were built alike. He needed to know the hot buttons to push on each person individually to get the most out of them. Some he could be direct and harsh with. Others he needed to critique one-on-one, in private. This approach minimized conflict and unneeded issues that could harm the team.

The Alvarez Approach

One of the primary keys to Barry Alvarez's success as a coach was his effective communication. As he states in his autobiography, *Don't Flinch*, *"You have to have a feel for your players. I think that's one of my strengths as a coach, and always has been. You have to know what buttons to push, when to push them, and when to back off."* [27]

The same approach was taken by another incredible person I speak about often, Major Dick Winters, whose leadership skills are on display in the HBO miniseries *Band of Brothers*. Of his leadership approach, Winters said in one of the episodes, *"Sometimes leadership is a matter of adjusting to the individual and you do this every day. You don't have one way of treating people; you adjust yourself to who you're talking to. I might talk to one person one way and someone else another."*

Cues for Effective Communication and Interaction

Here are some cues and tips to help you adapt to different DISC Behavior styles. Adapting is NOT changing who you are. It's simply avoiding unnecessary conflict by better connecting, communicating, and engaging with others.

Here are some practical tips when interacting with each DISC Behavioral Style (most of the following tips were taken from The Universal Language DISC Reference Manual) [28]

Maximizing Interactions with a HIGH D

When interacting with the High D Style, the key is to get to the point with direct, accurate, fact-based data.

Ways to Communicate with a High D

- Be clear, specific, and to the point—*Don't ramble on or waste their time.*

- Stick to business—*Don't try to build a personal relationship or chitchat.*

- Present the facts logically. Plan your presentation and approach efficiently—*Don't leave loopholes or cloudy issues if you don't want to be zapped.*

- Come prepared with all requirements, objectives, and support material in a well-organized package—*Don't forget or lose things, be unprepared, disorganized, or messy.*

- Provide alternatives and choices for making their own decisions—*Don't come with the decision made or make it for them.*

- Ask specific (preferably "what?") questions—*Don't ask rhetorical or useless questions.*

- Provide facts and figures about the probability of success or effectiveness of options—*Don't speculate wildly or offer guarantees and assurances where there is a risk in meeting them.*

- If you disagree, take issues with the facts—*Don't take issues with the High D personally.*

- Provide a win-win opportunity—*Don't force the High D into a losing situation.*

Ways to Motivate a High D

- Give them control of their own destiny and the destiny of others

- Give them the power and authority to achieve results

- Provide them with prestige, position, and titles

- Offer an expensive vehicle, money, and material things that indicate that success matters

- Provide an opportunity for rapid advancement

- Maintain their focus on the bottom line

- Follow the communication tips listed above, always

- Provide freedom from control, supervision, and details

- Ensure efficiency in people and equipment

- Afford new and varied experiences

- Create challenges with each task

- Initiate a forum for verbalizing

What Drives a High D

- Being direct

- Bullet-point information and approach

- Unique, cutting-edge ideas

- Competition, winning

Maximizing Interactions with a HIGH I

When interacting with the High I Style, the key is to be as personable, open, and friendly as possible. It is imperative to build rapport and a relationship.

Ways to Communicate with a High I

- Plan interactions that support their dreams and intentions— *Don't legislate and muffle.*

- Allow time for relating and socializing—*Don't be cold, curt, or tight-lipped.*

- Talk about people and their goals—*Don't bank on facts, figures, and alternatives.*

- Focus on people and action items. Put details in writing—*Don't leave decisions up in the air.*

- Ask for their opinion—*Don't be impersonal or task-oriented.*

- Provide ideas for implementing action—*Don't waste time in "dreaming."*

- Use enough time to be stimulating, fun, fast-moving—*Don't cut a meeting short or be too businesslike.*

- Provide testimonials from people they see as important or prominent—*Don't talk down to them.*

- Offer special incentives for their willingness to take risks—*Don't take too much time before you get to action items.*

Ways to Motivate a High I

- Provide an environment free from control and data

- Offer popularity and social recognition

- Encourage freedom of speech and people to talk to

- Create favorable working conditions

- Ensure group activities outside the job

- Encourage identification with a team

- Afford public recognition for their ability

- Offer monetary rewards

What Drives a High I

- Enthusiasm, rapport

- Benefits to people

- No heavy data or facts—personal is better

- Make them look good—compliment and appeal to their image

Maximizing Interactions with a HIGH S

When interacting with the High S Style, the key is to be patient and persistent, yet not overbearing. Let them move at their own pace.

Ways to Communicate with a High S

- Start with personalized comments and break the ice—*Don't rush headlong into business or the agenda.*

- Show sincere and honest interest in them as people—*Don't stick coldly or harshly to business.*

- Patiently draw out their personal goals and ideas. Listen and be responsive—*Don't force a quick response to your objectives.*

- Present your case logically, softly, and non-threateningly—*Don't threaten with personal power or be demanding.*

- Ask specific (preferably "How?") questions—*Don't interrupt as they speak. Listen carefully.*

- Move casually and informally—*Don't be abrupt and rapid in your pace.*

- If the situation impacts them personally, look for hurt feelings—*Don't mistake their willingness to go along for satisfaction.*

- Provide personal assurances and guarantees—*Don't promise something you cannot deliver.*

- If a decision is required of them, allow them time to think—*Don't force a quick decision; provide information.*

Ways to Motivate a High S

- Logical reasons to change

- Identification with team members

- Harmony—a happy home/work life balance

- Procedures that have been proven

- Closure on tasks

- Time to adjust to change

- Appreciation

- Recognition for a job well done

- Let them know you care

- Work in a small group of people and develop relationships

through collaboration and a collaborative environment

What Drives a High S:

- Be sincere and build trust
- Slow the pace; be methodical in approach
- Focus on collaboration—working together, team approach
- Give time to think things through

Maximizing Interactions with a HIGH C

When interacting with the High C Style, the key is to be cautious, patient, and very fact-oriented.

Ways to Communicate with a High C

- Prepare your case in advance—*Don't be disorganized or messy.*
- Approach in a direct and straightforward way—*Don't be casual, informal, or impersonal.*
- Present specifics and facts, and do what you say you can do—*Don't be vague about expectations or fail to follow through.*
- Use a thoughtful approach. Build credibility by looking at all sides of each issue—*Don't force a quick decision.*
- Draw up an Action Plan with scheduled dates and milestones—*Don't overpromise results; be conservative.*
- Take your time, but be persistent—*Don't be abrupt or rapid.*
- If you disagree, prove it with data and facts or testimonials from respected people—*Don't appeal to opinion or feelings as evidence.*
- Provide them with information and the time they need to make a decision.
- Allow them their space—*Don't be touchy-feely with them.*

Ways to Motivate a High C

- Provide operating procedures in writing

- Follow safety procedures
- Create ways to be part of a quality-oriented team
- Ensure no sudden or abrupt changes
- Afford reassurance that the job is being done correctly
- Ensure information and data that is available
- Create time to think
- Provide objective, tough problems to solve
- Provide manager who follows company policy

What Drives a High C

- Quality, service, and accuracy
- Dependability and trust
- Data, information, facts to analyze and consider
- Making good, safe decisions based on facts and reason

The above tips provide you with the roadmap you will need to successfully leverage interactions with others. It will eventually lead you to a deeper relationship with others by closing the communication gaps.

Keep in mind my comment earlier in this chapter that just because styles differ doesn't automatically mean that they clash or that there is a huge gap in communication. However, most gaps in communication occur when styles differ. This is common sense. The general rule of thumb is that alike styles tend to communicate and connect better. There is one interaction in alike styles where there could still be a bit of a gap. Any idea? Take a guess.

- D to a D?
- I to an I?
- S to an S?
- C to a C?

If you guessed the D to the D, you are correct. Since these styles are so aggressive, direct, and challenging, not to mention their conflict response is to fight, they are the styles that are most likely to clash amongst themselves.

If we can better understand ourselves and learn how to interact with others, we should significantly improve at dealing with the dicey issues that occur in our lives. Self-knowledge and self-awareness are keys in facing and overcoming adversity. If you can predict your interactions with others and improve them—the better off you'll be. You may even find that some people you struggled with in the past actually become friends, allies, or at least no longer a problem.

I know that's happened with me. I had several customers I dealt with during my days in corporate America like that. Before we knew and trusted each other, certain relationships started out rocky. However, when trust was built and communication aligned and improved, our relationships flourished. It can be the same for you too.

Now let's learn some more tips for becoming a champ in facing, overcoming, and learning from the adversity in our lives.

READER CALL TO ACTION

1. List 3-5 Key Takeaways/Learnings from Chapter 10.

2. Based on the exercise at the end of Chapter 4 and the cues for reading styles you learned in this chapter, what do you think is the DISC Style of the person?

   (To profile this person's style, review what you read in Chapter 4 and compare with what you now know about the 4-DISC Styles.)

   - What is their Primary DISC Style?

   - What is their Secondary DISC Style (if they have one)?

3. What is your DISC Style, and what are differences between you both? (Are there also similarities?)

4. List 3-5 things you can do to improve communication with them.

   - What are 3-5 potential "look-outs" between your style and theirs (things that may cause conflict/adversity)?

   - Profile others who you can improve relationships with and build the same action plan.

PART III
BUILD & MAINTAIN A
STRONG FOUNDATION

CHAPTER 11

DEVELOP & ACCESS A RESERVOIR OF OPTIONS

A tree with strong roots laughs at storms.

~

-Malay Proverb-

Planting Seeds and Strengthening the Roots

Essentially, this book is about creating your home, your foundation, and the solid ground to effectively maneuver through life, as well as how to address life's trials and tribulations in a proactive, productive manner. You want to learn to solve problems, not run from them or become discouraged by them. We just spent several chapters planting the seeds for success by accepting that adversity is a part of life, acknowledging that it is meant for us to evolve, and then taking a journey of self-discovery to help us understand our reactions to difficulties that arise.

So, the great question is: How do you continue to build this foundation? How do you re-establish an approach every day for successfully overcoming adversity in today's fast-paced, ever-changing environment? How can you learn to grind and rationally respond to adversity when prior experiences have been negative, limited, or even worse, non-existent? How can you achieve this when so many people who fear difficulties take the easy way out and feel a sense of entitlement?

The bottom line is that learning from life's experiences—both the good and the bad—sets the framework for future success. These experiences will serve a specific purpose for later things to come and provide the ability to access logical, rather than emotional, responses to situations. The key is to be prepared to analyze situations as you face them going forward. And, if possible, revisit past situations to apply what you've learned.

Leverage Past Success, Experiences, and Training

First, you must rely on any past success, training, and experience you've had that you can leverage to your advantage. I realized during my summer from hell that both the training my father had provided me, along with the first-hand experiences that I had working at the store, had laid the groundwork for me to be successful, despite his absence due to illness. This, in turn, allowed me to realize I had options. This realization enabled me to move from an emotional response to the situation (thinking my head was going to explode), to a more rational response (the sense of calm I experienced when I realized that I had what it took to run our store that crazy summer).

The key is to be able to effectively link current situations to past experiences or training. Obviously, the greater your reservoir of experiences, the more access to options you have at your disposal. The more options, the higher the propensity to face adversity proactively and productively. Lastly, even unsuccessful experiences, or failures of some sort, provide a learning. So if the event or situation didn't end positively, it still provided rich learning for how to turn those results around moving forward.

Creating a Reservoir of Options = Gaining Wisdom

My reservoir consists of both personal and business experiences. My personal reservoir enables me to access learnings from past scenarios pertaining to my personal life. Meanwhile, my business reservoir allows me to fall back on past scenarios and training in my professional life. Nearly every training program I've experienced over the past 30 years has added strength to my business and professional foundation.

Way back in my first job out of college, I learned a technique called "The 3-Fs" for handling customer objections. To this very day, whenever I hear an objection from a customer, I fall back on that technique. In fact,

I teach this to my current clients as well. Hence, when I or a client hear an objection from someone personally or professionally, I/they don't panic and experience the adrenaline rush. I/They fall back on a technique learned and practiced through experience and in training. This technique provides a foundation, a reservoir of options, that I and my clients can rely on. This skill and experience provides the pathway to realizing options, and in turn, proactively addresses the conflict for a more productive resolution.

BOOK TERMINOLOGY

Reservoir of Options—Part of overcoming adversity is the ability to respond rationally, logically, and purposefully. Part of that ability is realizing you have options to fall back on. A reservoir is having as many options as possible to rely on when adversity strikes. The more options, the greater the likelihood for success.

A Fertile Mind is a MUST

Essentially, I liken gaining such life experiences to gaining wisdom. The more experiences in life, both good and bad, the more wisdom we gain. This, however, needs to be accompanied through self-awareness and willingness to learn. Some people go through life oblivious to needed lessons that enable growth. To learn and gain wisdom we must approach life with a sense of curiosity and a strong willingness to learn and grow. Otherwise, we may be doomed to repeat the same mistakes over again.

This is yet another reason I think it is harmful to shield people, especially our youth, from difficulties. We're not providing opportunities to build the reservoir of experience and wisdom to succeed throughout life. Or, at the least, we're slowing the progression in their ability to evolve.

What if You Have Minimal Past Success, Experience, or Training?

You may be thinking, what if I don't have the experience or training to handle an adverse situation? What do I do now? First, you must change your outlook about adversity. Instead of panicking, you need to realize that this is an opportunity to learn, grow, and overcome—or at least to gain experience for future similar situations. Then you must begin building a foundation to both access past experiences, and also deal effectively with new ones. That is what we'll focus on going forward.

Revisiting the Three Parts of this Book

In revisiting where this book has taken you, let's review the content so far.

- **Part #1: Accept & Acknowledge** is about reminding us first that we must accept that adversity is a part of life and is not going away. Perhaps we can minimize, and often eliminate, unnecessary issues by following the strategies within this book. However, adversity as a whole is not going to be eliminated from your life. Secondly, we must acknowledge that adversity is meant for us to evolve into the people we were meant to become. Acceptance and acknowledgement are the first steps in preparing ourselves for success.

- **Part #2: Self-Discovery** is about understanding brain functionality and how it manifests in our lives, especially with regard to adversity. We learn how the brain functions specifically to us personally, and in our dealings with others. The key here is to create options. By understanding our personal style, we can better understand what triggers us and what our response will be. Once that knowledge is attained, we can better address adversity productively.

- **Part #3: Build & Maintain a Strong Foundation** is about creating and maintaining a foundation and awareness of the daily opportunities that manifest in our lives to strengthen our resolve in dealing with the trials of life. It's also about using each day as a chance to learn, grow, and develop into the people we were meant to become. Solidify the foundation. In addition, we can apply other skills to strengthen our resolve and build the roadmap to learn, face, and overcome obstacles.

Building the Reservoir of Options

The following recommendations act as a foundation to build a reservoir of options as an initial learning stage and as a storage facility later, with those experiences available to you when needed. The more resources and experiences you have and can document, the stronger you'll be handling future difficulties. Essentially, by building this reservoir, you're creating a roadmap for future adverse scenarios. And these scenarios, whether successful or not, will add to that reservoir of experience and options. The more robust our reservoir of options, the better our ability to access rational, reasoned responses to future adversity.

Develop a Learning Mindset.

Totally commit yourself to immediately beginning to view every day and situation you face as a chance to learn something new about events and yourself—having that fertile mind.

This may sound simplistic, but you need to begin opening yourself to the willingness to learn, raising your awareness that every day you can better yourself. If you don't take this approach to learning, you will hinder your development. Adversity is here to stay and is meant for us to evolve. Be observant of this fact and leverage it to your advantage. You can only do so if you're open to it and aware of it.

SAGE INSIGHTS

I view adversities, difficulties, and roadblocks as a means to learn and grow into being a stronger, more diverse individual. My immediate reaction to adversity is an intense feeling like wind is being taken out of my sails. I know in this exact moment I must stop, take a breath, and do and say nothing. I then take a look at the big picture and determine where are the lessons I'm supposed to learn and what steps do I need to take. The key is taking time and fully evaluating the situation without judging or reacting.

- *Lisa Sideris, Sr. Account Executive at a Big Four Accounting Firm*

Customize Your Approach

Most of the recommendations below and in the upcoming chapters can act as tools to keep you in that cortex-based rational mindset. Use all of those that will be recommended, or use those which resonate with you the most—also use other approaches not mentioned in this book that may indeed work for you. The key is to build a customized action plan that fits your needs, personality, and style the most. The more you can customize the approach, the more motivated you will be in taking the daily steps required to strengthen yourself.

I use a multitude of these recommendations based on my style and interests. The knowledge of my DISC Behavioral Style blend, along with implementation of many of these recommendations below, has changed my life immensely and helped me grow as a human being. I'm much more adept at dealing with the trials and tribulations in life.

The Situational Debrief Process

The Situational Debrief is a process for documenting and analyzing adverse situations, both past and present. The goal is to capture and absorb learnings from adverse experiences to prepare you for future scenarios. In other words, learn and grow from an adverse situation.

If you don't have a significant reservoir of experiences or relevant training to rely on, you may want to begin by documenting important past situations that reoccur as issues (for example, fearing change, dealing with a difficult person, interviewing for a job, panicking in the face of any adversity, etc.) You will want to recreate those experiences and analyze and view them positively, or at least as a learning tool to prepare you for future situations. Use this same process to learn from new situations you face. Here is a four-step Situational Debrief Process for journaling your findings for each experience:

- **Step #1: Capture the Situation.** Write down your current or past situation (an example of a past situation for me would be my summer from hell in Chapter 2). Don't stop with simply writing down the event. Get yourself to relive the moment. Put yourself in that spot, despite the difficulty ... and yes, it most likely will draw on emotions. You'll want to capture facts about the event so you can begin to think about it logically, not emotionally.

- **Step #2: Review the Outcomes.** Write down what the actual outcome of the situation is or was, whether good, bad, or indifferent. You want to identify what was adverse vs. desirable. This allows you to reconnect to both the good and bad of the event. In addition, it can help you recognize both the emotional trigger and emotional responses, if they occurred. This allows you to connect dots if handled emotionally (freeze/flight/fight), between what caused the response, and what was the response. The more you can recognize and connect the dots, the more likely you can recognize this habit in the future.

- **Step #3: Define Key Learnings.** Most importantly, capture what you learned from the event. This is the key to enabling you to step back from the emotion and logically analyze your situation, recreating positive experiences from something otherwise considered negative. Capture what you learned. What was good? What was hurtful, but not tragic? Did you learn anything at the time, and if not, what can you learn from it now? If there is some sort of foundational training, you can fall back on those as well. As an example, if you're in sales and are taught a "sales process" or skill, like handling objections, use this foundational training as the foundation to measure. Did you use the process or not? What did you do well or not so well based on the training you received?

- **Step #4: Identify Recommended Changes.** Once the key learning is identified, think about what you'd do differently the next time. Once again, step away from the emotion of it and think logically. You'll probably experience emotion as you revisit the situation, but hopefully not so intense that it overrules your rational thought process. The key point of the exercise is to redraw the experience in a positive light for future use in similar situations, using those learnings for potential future events. You've been there before, so you can handle it better next time.

A Proven Process—Personally & Professionally

This process does not represent a magic formula created by me. In fact, coaches, leaders, and managers have been using a similar process for years. In my first job out of college with Beecham Products, our managers used this process when working with sales reps at all levels. I've experienced it as rep and have used it for well over 30 years as a leader, coach, and manager with remarkable success.

Basically, when a sales rep made a call on a customer, the manager would simply observe. Whether the sales rep was using our sales process properly or not, whether they were doing well with the customer or not, the manager would sit back and simply observe. Then in the call afterward, the manager would lead a coaching debrief, asking the rep what went well and what didn't. Based on that dialogue, the manager responded accordingly, validating those things that went well, and those things that needed improvement, most often in a positive, upbeat manner.

The point was this: Every sales call was a learning opportunity, just as every experience in life is an opportunity to teach and reinforce fundamental skills required for success ion the job. Each call and coaching debrief prepared us for future calls, strengthening our likelihood for success, and preparing us for future roles in the company.

No Mistakes … Just Learnings

Basically, the sales reps learned through experiences, both good and bad. Then they used the same process with their respective teams when they were managers. Essentially, we were creating a reservoir of options and experiences that enabled us to grow and develop skills. And when adversity struck, we fell back on our experiences and training. I cannot tell you how many times I've faced obstacles and simply fell back on my experiences, learnings, and training for success … or at least found a learning or experience I could add to my reservoir of options.

This approach worked in spades. Despite the fact that our products at Beecham didn't carry near the market share of our main competitors, Procter & Gamble, and Colgate, we competed very well against them— all because of our training and coaching debrief process. We were called "the marines" of the consumer packaged goods industry. This is essentially the same approach for you to use in learning from the adversity in your lives.

Foundation for Success

I still use this process with my coaching clients. My two most influential mentors, Santo Laquatra and Meryl Moritz, use a similar approach in their coaching engagements as well. The bottom line is that every scenario is a learning opportunity to enable us to grow and evolve while strengthening our resolve for when lightning strikes. You now know your DISC Behavioral Style and how you deal with adversity. And now you also have a process, a foundation, and a reservoir of options for when it strikes.

SAGE INSIGHTS

I have the habit (and I coach my client to cultivate this as a practice, if relevant) of doing a written postmortem. What happened? How did I handle it? What worked, what didn't? What resources did I have that I could have availed myself of? What resources do I lack and need to build up to have sufficient reserves to deal with adversity in future? This helps me build the new map for thinking through tough times.

- Meryl Moritz, Master Certified Coach at Meryl Moritz Resources

Next Steps

Now that the foundation for building a reservoir of options has been laid, we can continue to build on these learnings. Every day is essentially an opportunity to learn, grow, and develop ourselves. The key is to not only continue falling back on that foundation, but also secure it and make it stronger. By developing hobbies, habits, and taking initiative, we can strengthen ourselves for the future.

READER CALL TO ACTION

1. List 3-5 Takeaways/Learnings from Chapter 11.

2. Revisit an adverse situation you've faced and use the Situational Debrief from this chapter:
   (Focus on a situation you either <u>failed, struggled</u> and/or which <u>didn't turn out as expected.</u>)

   - Capture the Situation

   - Review the Outcomes

   - Define Key Learnings

   - Identify Recommended Changes

3. Revisit an adverse situation you've faced and use the Situational Debrief from this chapter:
   (Focus on a situation in which you <u>succeeded</u> or <u>benefitted</u> from the outcome.)

   - Capture the Situation

   - Review the Outcomes

   - Define the Key Learnings

   - Identify Recommended Changes

CHAPTER 12

STRENGTHENING THE FOUNDATION

If I had six hours to chop down a tree, I'd spend the first four sharpening my ax.

~

-Abraham Lincoln-

Lesson from a Master

One of my favorite life changing books is Stephen Covey's *The 7 Habits of Highly Effective People*. The entire book is outstanding. However, my favorite insights come from the chapter that focuses on Habit #7, **Sharpen the Saw**. The insights from this chapter feed well into the content in the chapter of this book. We laid the foundation creating a reservoir of options in the previous chapter. Now, what are those daily habits we can establish to build on that foundation? These habits also tie into acceptance and acknowledgement—adversity is going to happen, and it is meant for us to evolve—as well as opportunities to grow specific to our respective DISC Behavior Style. In essence, this chapter is building on everything this book has covered so far.

Sharpen the Saw

Per Covey, "Sharpen the Saw" means preserving and enhancing the greatest asset you have—you. It means having a balanced program for self-renewal in the four areas of your life: physical, social/emotional, mental, and spiritual.

As you renew yourself in each of the four areas, you create growth and change in your life. Sharpen the Saw keeps you fresh so you can continue to practice the other six habits. You increase your capacity to produce and handle the challenges around you. Without this renewal, the body becomes weak, the mind mechanical, the emotions raw, the spirit insensitive, and the person selfish.

Feeling good doesn't just happen. Living a life in balance means taking the necessary time to renew yourself. It's all up to you. You can renew yourself through relaxation, or you can totally burn yourself out by overdoing everything. You can pamper yourself mentally and spiritually, or you can go through life oblivious to your well-being. You can experience vibrant energy, or you can procrastinate and miss out on the benefits of good health and exercise. You can revitalize yourself and face a new day in peace and harmony, or you can wake up in the morning full of apathy because your get-up-and-go has got-up-and-gone. Just remember that every day provides a new opportunity for renewal, a new opportunity to recharge yourself instead of hitting the wall. All it takes is the desire, knowledge, and skill.[29]

Strengthening the Foundation

This book offers some similar insights that may be found in Covey's Habit #7. However, the emphasis in this book is gleaned not only from my personal experiences, but also that of the many individuals whom I interviewed and surveyed for this book. These people are highly successful in their own right, so obviously I wanted to know their habits and hobbies, specifically around learning, facing, and overcoming adversity. Their insights are meant to help you in your journey. I'm sure you use some of these already and may have some not listed here. The key is to provide you with new insights and opportunities to develop and strengthen yourself so you can continue to evolve through life, especially in the face of obstacles.

4-Part Strengthening of Foundation Steps

Every day offers us the opportunity to face, learn, overcome obstacles, and strengthen our resolve. So far, this book has provided the pathway to do just that. However, that is not the end. Every day we must be aware and prepared to learn and grow. Just because the foundation of a house is laid doesn't mean it won't eventually crumble. Remember my summer from hell story? A foundation may need upkeep, fixes, additions, and reinforcement. That is what strengthening the foundation is all about.

The next four parts in this book speak just to that point. They include habits, hobbies, tasks, and support mechanisms we can leverage every day to ensure we're strong and successful, especially when adversity strikes. In other words, this chapter is about strengthening ourselves for when those adverse situations manifest. In Covey's terms, this is this book's version of Sharpen the Saw, or renewal.

#1: Support Yourself

The key aspect of supporting yourself is to find a network of people you can rely on to help develop either personally and/or professionally. These people can also help you in times of turmoil. These are people you can trust with providing strong advice and unbiased insights. These are people who best know you and look out for your best interest, yet are willing to be open, honest, and direct as well. The operative word here is TRUST! These are people you trust and value. Obviously, family is an excellent first approach, if they can offer such unbiased, honest, positive support. Some families can, some cannot. So having external options is equally important. Here are a few recommendations:

- **Hire a Coach or Leverage a Mentor (or Therapist)**. I've hired a coach at various times in my life, depending on my specific needs. I also have several mentors, people I can contact to share ideas, vent, and ask for opinions. Several are actually former coaches and managers. These are a group of folks I turn to for help in setting positive patterns, to ensure I handle dicey situations in a productive, rational manner. It's always great to have various ears at your disposal, good people that you trust who will provide good guidance and insights you may not see on your own. My main mentor is a man named Santo, whom I've gone to for many years. He's excellent at listening, and always gives spot-on advice. He's blunt—brutally honest. I can always lean on him for honest insights. In addition, I act as a coach/ mentor to many of my clients. In fact, executive/ managerial/ sales/ personal/ professional coaching is a core part of my work, and I love it as it allows me to work one-on-one with people in situations specific to them. No situation is alike and I love the challenge.

I've also hired personal coaches several times during corporate my career. They were especially helpful in guiding me through tough times. Possibly the toughest was helping me transition from the corporate world to start my consulting business many years ago. For that process, I actually used two different coaches at various times, and their support and insights were invaluable. Their insights gave me the courage to walk "cold turkey" from a highly secure corporate job to a riskier world of business ownership. It was a risk that reaped great rewards. And I couldn't have done it without the coaches and mentors who've supported me through the years. I'm a primary High S, so big changes are not easy for me. So having coaches know that was key as well.

Obviously, its key for a coach/mentor to know and understand your DISC Behavior Style. As reviewed in Chapter 10, various styles of people can clash and create more issues. You need to have a coach that meshes best with you and/or at least understands your style.

I've played sports my entire life, and those coaches that meshed best with me appealed to my High S style. I didn't enjoy the Type A personality coaches ... I enjoyed the coaches who could communicate with me one-on-one in a non-threatening manner. It didn't mean they couldn't be harsh with me. It was their approach that made the difference. And not only did they resonate better with me, I responded in kind with my performance as well. I had the best success in sports with those coaches who approached me properly. You need to do the same. Find coaches/mentors who can get the best out of you based on your style.

SAGE INSIGHTS

Having a core group of confidants to whom I can tell anything without fear of judgment or reprisal has saved me from shutting down or shutting a door that could profitably remain open. I am reminded of many aphorisms my long-time mentor shared with me in tough times. 'What we resist persists.' 'Our pre-disposition determines our disposition.' These short reminders come back to me, encouraging me to keep on keepin' on.

- Meryl Moritz, Master Certified Coach at Meryl Moritz Resources

- **Observe and Model Other Successful People.** Every day offers us opportunities to observe and model successful people. Through observation we learn how to be successful at various things. When I interviewed Barry Alvarez, he stated that he had often observed his Uncle Jon when he worked at his grocery store. According to Alvarez, his Uncle Jon had excellent people skills. He could schmooze the loyal customers, but at the same time deal harshly but successfully with bad customers or vendors. Barry's observations of his uncle helped him hone his people skills and it paid off in spades. Alvarez is known as a great motivator and people person. He was an excellent recruiter of college athletes as well. How else could he have turned Wisconsin's football program around from perennial losers to winners in a few short years? This was in large part due to his strong people skills, very much honed during his years working at his Uncle Jon's small store.

Per Alvarez, he had another huge mentor, Pat McGraw. "I grew up in a small town in western Pennsylvania where athletics was the most important thing in my life," Alvarez said. "My high school football coach was my baseball coach, and he was very important to me ... He influenced me so much I decided that's all I wanted to do with my life."

Adoni Maropis' role models were his dad, mom, brothers, and his cousins, Pete and Mike Maropis. He learned many valuable skills from observing all of them. As he said, "I never had to leave the dinner table to find my role models."

Pete Stracci modeled the work ethic of his mother. We all have people who we can observe to become better people, not only in our daily learning, but especially those who can teach us lessons on overcoming difficulties. This includes people like my former coach Eric Parker, who taught me about the limbic system and cortex, emotional and rational responses to adversity.

Every day offers us the opportunity to learn from others, both good things, and bad. What to do, what not to do. Most importantly, we can learn from anyone at any time, we just have to be observant. We need to raise that knowledge and realize that every day, everyone offers us a chance to learn, grow, and develop. In addition, it's especially important if that person exhibits skills you desire, much like Barry and his Uncle.

- **Subscribe to Blog/ Podcasts/ You Tube/ Social Media Videos.** You can also find mentors, coaches, and conduct observations virtually. There are literally hundreds of people and sites you can view to help motivate and strengthen you. Find topics and people who inspire, motivate, and educate you. When your mind is focused on that which is good, you'll be surprised at the outcome, and especially how that frame of mind helps you during adversity—as Eric Parker would say, "keeps you in the cortex."

I know a popular influencer with the athletes at my martial arts gym is entrepreneur "You Tuber" Gary Vaynerchuk. I have several favorite influencers that I enjoy watching including Tony Robbins, Stephen Covey, and the late Wayne Dyer. I'll watch them anytime, in any venue they appear. They not only provide me with much needed inspiration and motivation, but with valuable insights into topics that are of specific interest to me.

#2: Invest in Yourself

The next way to secure your personal foundation is to invest in your own growth and development, both as a release but also as a way of ensuring you grow and succeed in life, especially in the midst of difficulties. This is especially good if you want to strengthen yourself in areas that need it. If you think you're missing a particular skill or knowledge that is hindering you or causing you difficulties, address it. If you can shore up these areas, you might be better able to deal with adverse situations. Or possibly, if this skill is enhanced, perhaps you'll be more willing to step out of your comfort zone and try something you otherwise would not have tried. This opens up the valuable reservoir of options you'll need to keep growing in the face of challenges, but also gain sense of satisfaction and confidence—both of which bode well for your evolution as a human being. Some possible ideas to help you invest in yourself:

- **Take Personal Educational/Learning Seminars.** Take classes that will broaden your personal development. Learn new skills you're either interested in or that can strengthen needed areas. If you have a fear of speaking, take a class to enable you to practice speaking skills in a friendly environment. If you're not technologically astute, take a class to increase your knowledge. There are so many options. Go learn a language or get your bachelor or master's degree; the options are unlimited. In this day and age, there should be no excuses not to take advantage of such learning and growth opportunities.

- **Take Professional Development/Learning Seminars.** All of these personal development classes can also apply to your professional world. If your company offers internal developmental classes, seek them out and take them. If your company has funds for outside training, then also take that opportunity. If you really desire to become better at a given skill, then make the time investment in yourself either by taking a class, hiring a coach, or watching a seminar online.

If your company has a minimal budget and you need to learn a relevant professional skill, make the investment yourself. What is the dollar value in an investment into your career versus the emotional stress of struggling through a job, being stressed and possibly fired, or quitting and being unemployed? Think of the adverse situations that will manifest themselves in that situation. In other words, the investment in yourself is more than worth it.

If you're interviewing for a new job, ask the hiring managers about their training and development programs. If they don't commit to the development of their people, that will tell you a great deal about the company and its potential commitment to you as a long-term employee.

- **Invest in Training for Your Business/Company.** For corporate leaders, entrepreneurs, and business owners, spend time and money on training and development for your employees. This investment not only provides a foundation for success, but also allows people to draw on their new knowledge as they experience real-world situations, building the experiences that they can rely on to operate a maximum capacity. This investment will lead to huge benefits for you and your organization. This book is about foundations, creating a reservoir of options for people to rely on when difficulties strike. Wouldn't you want your people appropriately prepared to deal with real world issues they face working for you? It makes total sense that investment in your people pays off.

Bottom line, if you have a happy, well-trained organization, you can at least minimize adversity and unneeded headaches. An investment in your employees is a peace of mind investment for you. If you're still not convinced that the investment in your people is worth it, check out the stats in this graphic:

Training & Development Benefits

➤ Invest in Your Employees

- Happy employees are productive employees
- There is a cost to unhappy employees
- A loss of a good employee is even costlier
- Spend the time required to develop your talent

➤ Training & Development Works

- An article in *Public Personnel Management* revealed the following in a study
  - Training increased productivity by over 22%
  - Training with coaching increased productivity by 88%
- A study in *Manchester Review* revealed that companies that invest in coaching receive an ROI of more than five times

---

#3: Test Yourself

The next step is to test yourself by placing yourself in slightly uncomfortable situations. To be clear, by uncomfortable I'm not saying dangerous. I'm saying stretch yourself beyond previously thought capacities. By stretching yourself, you're creating those experiences that you can draw on for future adverse situations. If I'm in an emotional state and I freeze when a lot of change is occurring, I'm going to struggle big time. If I can put myself in those scenarios and stay in that rational, cortex-based state of mind, I can learn it feels like, and use it as an opportunity to grow. I'm not saying all of a sudden I'm a change agent and now love it. I'm saying I come to realize that I can deal with such situations rationally. I can get through it, learn, and address the situation as productively as I can. I DO NOT need to freeze or stay frozen in the event. This learning experience creates an experience and a reservoir of options for me. So, with that said …

- **Accept Change and Take Risks.** Once again, I'm not saying life-threatening or dangerous risks. But be willing to step out into the unknown. What's the worst thing that can happen? You might just learn something, and that can begin the series of experiences that enables you to limit your emotional responses when something throws you off in the future. In addition, if you've developed the learning mindset and you've documented adverse situations, this will add to a reserve of options, experiences, and trainings you can rely on in the future.

In addition, most often risk and acceptance of change can produce great results. In the opening chapter, I mentioned the story of my friend Adoni Maropis and his role in the TV show *24*. What actually transpired on that first day on the set is interesting.

Prior to stepping on the set of *24*, Adoni did a great deal of research on the role to really get into the character. He also had his lines memorized down pat. Once he arrived, Kiefer Sutherland said he wanted Adoni to read for him. Upon listening to Adoni deliver his lines as the villain Fayed, Sutherland said, "You do that very well, but we need to change and cut out a bit of dialogue and also move a lot of lines around. Are you okay with that?"

Adoni was flabbergasted and frustrated. He simply replied, "Sure, no problem." He thought he'd nailed it and now had to, again, start from scratch. Now, any slight change in a script can really throw an actor off, especially after all the work put into memorizing a monologue of three or four pages. The pressure and challenge was on. Adoni now had a short time to prepare for his scene with Sutherland.

However, upon further review while alone, Adoni realized that Sutherland's recommended changes were spot-on, and in fact made that scene significantly better. So, as Adoni said, a pressure- packed, risky change ended up paying off in spades, as they both nailed their roles for that given episode, and the season. In addition, Adoni stretched himself as an actor which helped him further hone his craft.

- **Be Willing to Face Adversity.** Adversity is a part of life and it occurs to help you grow. So, the more you face it and learn from it, the more you'll grow and be prepared for it in the future. Once again, a learning mindset and documenting situations helps here. Notice how each step builds on the previous one. This book starts off with accepting that adversity is NOT going away. Can it be minimized? Sure, but you want to do that in a positive way, not by hiding from it or avoiding it. This book also covered the acknowledging that adversity is meant for us to evolve ... if you accept and acknowledge both premises and follow the insights and directions in this book, facing adversity going forward should be quite different for you ... it's a learning opportunity, not a deterrence.

- **Stretch Yourself/Be Willing to Fail.** In my opinion, there are so many more learning points to be gleaned during failure. Being open to failure or difficulty is what this book is about. Accept that adversity will not go away, nor will failure. You're going to fail or not succeed in life, face it— it's a fact; so, why not learn and grow from it? The worse that can happen is a lesson learned, and experiences drawn from it.

I attempt to stretch myself all the time, both personally and professionally. That can be hard as I'm a High S, and if you remember, High S's don't necessarily like change; they enjoy the status quo or if they do change, it's typically at a slower pace. Knowing this about myself, I make a conscious effort to push myself. I have to or I'll become stagnant. In fact, writing this book was one of those efforts. I firmly believe in and love this book topic. I think it is hugely important, especially in this day and age. In addition, I wanted to pay homage to my hometown as it's a great story to share ... once again, especially in this day and age.

However, I can find the process of writing very tedious. I'm decent at getting a foundation for a book or article laid, but taking it to the next level can get tedious and frustrating. The effort is an emotional rollercoaster for me as I have moments of excitement and gratification, but at other times suffer doubt and worry about whether it is good enough. But overall, this process strengthens me. It gives me yet another opportunity to challenge myself, to step into the uncomfortable, to learn and grow. It also forces me to remain in the cortex, stay rational, clear-headed, and not let the emotions run away. I realize the benefits far outweigh the struggle of doing it. It is yet another growing process for me, and most importantly, people will hopefully benefit from it.

Many successful managers and leaders offer the opportunity to fail. Eric Parker, who manages a large team, says he opens the door for his team to fail. It provides them with learnings. They take a fearless approach because now the worst pain is a lesson to be applied to experience and that reservoir of options. On the flip side, elimination of fears greatly increases the opportunity for success as well. Creating an open, safe environment is refreshing and rewarding at the same time.

#4: Refresh Yourself

The last step is finding habits or hobbies that help you become more productive and aware of yourself. These can include learning new things, once again stretching yourself, and building your rational thinking muscles. It also includes getting yourself healthy physically, mentally, spiritually, and emotionally. These offer us the chance to gain access and strengthen that reservoir of options.

- **Self-Affirmations/Prayer.** These are positive statements (self-scripts) that can condition your subconscious mind to help you develop a more positive perception of situations and yourself, thereby driving rational, reasoned thinking. Affirmations can help you to change harmful behaviors and accomplish goals. They can also help undo the damage caused by negative scripts, those things you repeatedly tell yourself or that others repeatedly tell you that contribute to a negative self-perception. They can help calm you and keep you in a relaxed frame of mind, versus having unhelpful emotional responses of freeze, flight, fight. Affirmations are easy to create and use; they require only dedication to make them work. Some examples of positive affirmations:

- I think positively, take responsibility for my actions, and create my own future.

- Opportunities always come my way. I seize them and accomplish my objectives.

- Adversity is a normal part of life to help me grow and become a better person.

- I am motivated, optimistic, and solution-oriented.

- I make my own choices and I create my own future.

- I set and achieve goals easily. I am an achiever.

These self-affirmations can include prayer as well. I don't care what your religious beliefs are, prayer can always provide peace of mind. When you have peace, you have a clear mind and this enables you to deal with things rationally and logically as they occur during the day. I pray several times a day. Sometimes, I say the exact same prayer several times a day, or sometimes I use one more relevant to a given situation. It's the perfect way for me start and end the day, while keeping me balanced and mindful. As Tony Robbins calls it a "beautiful state."

Bottom line, affirmations and prayer keep me grounded. Sometimes the grind of life can be trying, but having a solid foundation and a clear head is key. It's something to keep you firm and grounded when the proverbial sh*t hits the fan ... which is sure to happen.

- **Read Motivational/Positive Material.** Surround yourself with positive insights of others; in fact, drown yourself in them. A great deal of my success is drawn from my readings. Stephen Covey's *The Seven Habits of Effective People*, James Allen's *As a Man Thinketh*, and the Bible have been huge influences on my life. So have many of Tony Robbins' seminars and motivational quotes. Another great resource are the great people throughout history. I've learned much from the lives and leadership of Winston

Churchill, Abraham Lincoln, and Dick Winters, leader of *Band of Brothers*. The owner of my martial arts gym, Matt Arroyo, listens to about 25-30 motivational, self-development audio books a year. He recommends his athletes do the same. So it's no wonder his gym in Gracie Tampa South is known as one of the best martial arts schools in the USA.

- **Read Motivational Quotes Daily.** These have always been a grounding tool for me. In fact, I've been offering free motivational quotes to thousands of people, both via social media and Constant Contact, for years. It's not only uplifting for me, as I get to read and peruse the quotes daily as I select them, but the feedback I receive from recipients is uplifting, too. There is nothing more gratifying than having a stranger email me saying they needed that quote today, or just a simple "thank you." This helps keep me grounded, but also heartens me that I've helped someone else that given day. It serves two powerful purposes. Use motivational quotes for yourself, but also don't ever hesitate to send quotes to others who may appreciate them. It's well worth it, I promise. Getting out of our own skin does wonders for putting life in perspective. As they say, it's often better to give than receive.

- **Get Healthy Physically.** One of the best way to handle life's difficulties is to get healthy. Let's face it: If we're not healthy, that in and of itself can cause unnecessary and unknowing additional adversity. Heart disease, diabetes, etc. are all life threatening and can cause serious issues, hindering both our ability to deal with daily issues and our enjoyment of life. I highly recommend increasing physical activity. In many ways, that clears our mind, body, and spirit as well. By increasing physical activity, you'll create experiences and receive training that will better enable you to employ logical, rational thinking, and further prepare you for future issues.

Per an article in *Fast Company* called "What Happens to Our Brains When We Exercise and How It Makes Us Happier," there is a scientific reason why if you start exercising, your brain recognizes that as a moment of stress. As your heart rate increases, the brain thinks you are either fighting the enemy or fleeing from it. To protect yourself and your brain from stress, you release a protein called BDNF (Brain-Derived Neurotrophic Factor). This BDNF has a protective and also reparative element for your memory neurons and acts as a reset switch. That's why we often feel so at ease after exercising; things are clear and we're eventually happy.

At the same time, endorphins, another chemical to fight stress, are released in your brain. Your endorphins' main purposes are, according to researcher McGovern:

These endorphins tend to minimize the discomfort of exercise, block the feeling of pain and are even associated with a feeling of euphoria.[30]

Lastly, and on the flipside, it's equally important to have recovery time if you are a workout-a-holic. If you overwork or train too intensely, that can have negative repercussions like injuries, which throw you off-track and can frustrate. I've learned to combine different types of workouts to not overstress my body, but I also take downtime when I think it's needed.

- **Learn Martial Arts.** Martial arts are an excellent way to help us better face obstacles on a daily basis. First and foremost, they teach discipline, both physically and mentally. Second, you learn about defeat often and how to handle it. Martial arts feed into the ability to learn to handle adversity rationally, not over-emotionally. You learn skills daily and practice them in real-world scenarios constantly. You learn about defeat and apply learnings for improvement. The improvement is both rewarded in self-gratification and belt rewards. The more you improve, the higher belt you can achieve. Ultimately, you become a master in that art form, also known as a black belt.

I'm a recent convert to martial arts and am addicted. After many years of saying I wanted to try a form of martial arts, I finally started kickboxing about five years ago and it became a passion. I find the workout demanding, but greatly rewarding as well. The kickboxing discipline I focus on is Muay Thai, also known as Thai Boxing, and The Art of Eight Limbs. You use hands, elbows, knees, and feet. In addition to an outstanding workout, it really enhances mental capacity. And in my opinion, it's gratifying emotionally and spiritually as well. I cannot describe the satisfaction after a hard session with Coaches Kru Dan Rawlings and Billy Quarantillo.

Another martial art that is incredibly rewarding physically and mentally is Brazilian jiu-jitsu (aka BJJ). BJJ is a form of grappling that is highly strategic, almost a physical chess match, so to speak. Those who practice BJJ not only learn skills, but growth through failure. Believe me, when doing BJJ you don't win all the time. In fact, you most often lose, and it can be quite humbling. But it's an incredible learning experience, with huge growth potential for those who practice it.

SAGE INSIGHTS

My hobby to help with adversity and clear my mind is Brazilian jiu-jitsu. Sometimes the best thing you can do when you have adversity is to detach from it for a day or two and get your mind onto something else. It is impossible to spar in BJJ and think about your problems at the same time. Then, once you get that great sweat and the endorphins are flowing, you always tend to feel better. Einstein once said, "We cannot solve our problems with the same thinking we used when we created them." BJJ gets you in a different mind frame.

- Matt Arroyo, Brazilian Jiu-Jitsu black belt, coach, entrepreneur, and former UFC athlete

Learning martial arts will teach you to grind. It will do wonders in strengthening your ability to effectively deal with the adversity life throws at you. You also learn great attributes practicing martial arts, such as discipline, patience, perseverance, humility, and integrity.

In my opinion and experience, martial artists are salt-of-the-earth people. Dedicated, helpful, gracious, welcoming—I'm sure not all martial arts schools create such positive environments, but in my experience, most do. Find one that does, and you'll not only improve your life, but meet some great people. I'd also recommend children get started in martial arts early. They will build their confidence, learn skills, meet new people, and learn how to deal with adversity at a young age. Many martial arts schools focus on how to handle bullies non-violently.

- **Yoga.** Another excellent way to calm the mind, to prepare for the craziness of life, is to practice yoga. I've practiced yoga over the years, but have really hit it heavily the last year or so. Not only does yoga provide obvious physical benefits through stretching, balance, and agility, but it also is an excellent form of relaxation and centering of the mind. I do various forms of hot yoga that I find both intense and relaxing. In addition, the hot yoga has improved my Muay Thai, mainly in terms of flexibility and balance. They work well together and give me needed benefits physically, but also mentally, spiritually, and emotionally.

SAGE INSIGHTS

The practice of yoga allows me the opportunity to reset my mind and nervous system. It's a call to prayer moment where my body, mind, and breath are reminded to act in unison. That practice then follows me off the mat and how I breathe through a challenging pose is mirrored in how I handle a challenging moment in life.

Yoga itself is the science of well-being and uses the functions of the body to tell the body how to feel. You increase oxygenation, lower your blood pressure, activate digestion, detoxify, release lactic acid, and strengthen the muscles while elongating them, leaving you a more flexible person emotionally and physically.

Yoga releases happy hormones like dopamine into your system and leaves you a better version of yourself. It's that clarity of mind that is required for any meaningful overcoming of adversity. The goal is not to win, to beat adversity. The goal is to react to it in a way that makes its existence laughable.

- *Roni Sloman, Certified Life Coach and founder, owner of Bella Prana Yoga Studio*

- **Focus on Selflessness.** One of the best ways to stay refreshed, be less overwhelmed, and grow as a human being is to give of yourself. Volunteer or get involved in a cause you find worthy. I'm fortunate that my business, albeit not volunteer, allows me the ability to help people every single day. I'm a coach, trainer, and consultant, so I live, eat, drink, and breathe personal professional development in myself and others. I'm also considering a non-profit business as well. The fact that my business focuses in helping people is so rewarding and has helped me in so many ways. I'm fortunate enough to get paid for it. Through the years I've done volunteer work for Big Brothers and an organization called SERVE which focused on speaking to kids in high-risk schools. Both of these changed my life and were major experiences that propelled me into the training and development world in which I'm currently engaged.

The bottom line is helping others takes attention off of ourselves. I'm not saying our needs don't need to be met, but spending time helping others, volunteering, even complimenting others, has a naturally uplifting and motivating effect. The more we can serve others, the less we think about ourselves. And in a counterintuitive way, we end up helping ourselves, too. The reservoir of experiences and options we can gain definitely feeds into our abilities to be less emotional, more confident, reasoned, and rational when difficulties strike. And due to your service to others, you just never know what guardian angel could be by your side in time of need.

Combining All Resources

Referring back once again to Chad Hymas, I asked him what habits he applies to keep him mindful, and in his terms, keep that lens focused on that which is good, not bad. He said he starts every day with the following four steps.

- He meditates for at least 10 minutes (prayer or affirmation)

- He does something physical

- He calls his wife, essentially to thank her for being okay with him being on the road traveling so much (showing gratitude, which is covered in the next chapter)

- He makes it a point to compliment many people he meets throughout the day

As you can see, he combines several of the aforementioned tools to help him stay grounded or renewed, so to speak. This enables him to start his day on a very positive note. This grounding process helps to ensure that he views adversity with the proper lens.

Enhancing the Reservoir of Options

Lastly, these foundation strengthening recommendations also grow our reservoir of options. The more we learn, grow, and experience, the more options we create for ourselves when adversity strikes. The families in my hometown of Burgettstown used adversity as a stepping stone for their success and that of their families. Their vast array of experiences—both good and bad—provided them with a reservoir of options. They didn't have safety nets or excuses. They learned to grind! This same theory holds for you as well. Seek all opportunities to create those pathways of success and experience. Nurture wisdom and also be grateful for the opportunity to learn and grow with each and every day, which is precisely our next topic.

READER CALL TO ACTION

1. List 3-5 Key Takeaways/Learnings from Chapter 12.

2. List affirmative steps you can take to **Support Yourself.**

   - By what date?

3. List affirmative steps you can take to **Invest in Yourself.**

   - By what date?

4. List affirmative steps you will take to **Test Yourself.**

   - By what date?

5. List affirmative actions you will take to **Refresh Yourself.**

   - By what date?

CHAPTER 13

LIFE'S CLASS IS ALWAYS IN SESSION; ALWAYS BE ATTENTIVE AND GRATEFUL

I never lose. Either I win or I learn.

~

-Conor McGregor-

Daily Opportunities for Growth

Every day provides the opportunity for us to grow and develop as human beings who learn more about ourselves, our style, our triggers, and our emotional responses. Every day offers the opportunity to hone the skill of accessing rational thinking to address adversity in a productive, proactive manner. Every day offers us the chance to apply new experiences on how to deal with our trials and tribulations, further strengthening the reservoir of options to handle problems. So, if you start looking at every day as an opportunity and are grateful for that opportunity, good results are sure to come.

Turning Points—Learning Points

The most powerful situations for growth that have occurred in my life have all occurred around some of the most difficult times. Nearly all my struggles have played a role in my growth as a human, and also supplied me with ways to leverage these situations positively in the future. In fact, one of the cornerstones of my business originated from the most difficult situation during my 20-year career in corporate America (discussed next). I have leveraged that difficult situation in my current business with a workshop, keynote, and one-on-one coaching. In other words, that situation was placed in my life to be used later in my world as a consultant. If it hadn't happened, or I hadn't addressed it properly (emotionally vs. rationally), it would be of no such value to me now.

Just So You Know, They Hate Kodak

It was roughly 18 years into my career when I was looking for a new transition, something to really test the skills I had acquired working in corporate America. An opportunity to test those skills appeared within Eastman Kodak. It was a big job, where I got to lead a team of five sales reps calling on a very large, influential, and highly successful food retailer with well over 50% of the New York/New Jersey metro market share. It was a lot of responsibility with a high-volume retailer and an opportunity to leverage all the skillsets in my arsenal of experience. It was quite an interesting opportunity—and perfectly timed—as it could test my skills in several ways.

The Tony Soprano of Retailers

My customer, the large food retailer, had a reputation for being very difficult for sales people to deal with. The horror stories of dealing with their buyers were the stuff of legend. In fact, after my experiences with them, I'd say calling on them was like calling on the Sopranos. The only difference was that Tony would kill you and the pain would be over. With this customer, you had to keep going back for more. The recruiter provided me with an interesting warning, one that proved to be quite accurate and made me wish that I had been dealing with Tony Soprano instead!

This ended up being my toughest job and was my most difficult client in those 20 years of corporate America. The situation was so bad that before taking the job, I was told by the recruiter who had contacted me and my boss that this customer "hated Kodak." Well, I took the job and found out quickly that the recruiter and my boss were correct. The customer hated Kodak! The relationship was deeply strained; our business was in the tank; and they looked at me like I was the enemy. They were very angry at us because they believed we weren't giving them the best prices for our product. Essentially, they thought we were giving better price deals to their competition, which we weren't. The way they operated their business and structured our promotions led to the price discrepancies. It was brutal. I was getting nasty calls daily, and the intensity multiplied. They really tested my limbic system emotional response of both freeze and fight! It was very difficult.

Déjà vu—I've Been Prepared to Handle This Situation

However, after several months, I started making inroads, gaining trust, and getting wins. First, I fell back on all my training and past experiences leading up to this point. Just like the story of my house collapsing, I realized I had options. My past experiences and training prepared me for this situation. I found that sense of peace and confidence. I remained rational, not emotional. Because of this, I found way to think outside the box and provide them with programs to drive their business and beat their competition. In fact, we ended up growing their business by double digits in an industry that was in decline. I went from enemy to partner, from vendor to consultant, and this completely changed the dynamic of our relationship.

A Happy Ending—Positive Results, and Valuable Lessons

Within the year, I'd turned that absolutely horrible situation around. What began as my worst job and toughest client ended up being my greatest success story in a rather stellar 20-year career prior to opening my consulting business. In fact, I use this story as an example with my current clients, both in workshops and keynotes. It's as though this difficult situation prepared me to grow my consulting business, too. This allotted me with new learning and insights to not only help me grow my business, but more importantly, to assist my current clients. They all LOVE that story, and the knowledge and insights resonate with them. In other words, my clients and I are still reaping the benefits of that difficult situation.

An Important Stepping Stone … It Was Meant to Happen

I firmly believe that particular job situation was meant to happen—it was to prepare me for bigger and better things. In addition, it taught me a great deal about myself and my response to adversity. As I said, I tend to shut down and freeze, which I did often. But I fought through those emotions and worked diligently to keep my composure, stay rational, and find solutions. I had a reservoir of options that I previously didn't think I had. Because I stayed cool in the face of the greatest work adversity I'd ever faced, I found solutions for both the client and Kodak. In addition, that situation provided yet another incredible experience at overcoming obstacles by also creating a future reservoir of options for the future, namely my current consulting business and my personal life.

SAGE INSIGHTS

Adversity is a great teacher. If you're willing to learn from mistakes, or any difficult situation, it will prepare you for future success. Adversity is an opportunity to get myself and my players focused on the ultimate goal and overcome the next roadblock on our way to excellence.

- Jay Hayes, Defensive Line Coach with the Tampa Bay Buccaneers

Life is a Classroom—Observe, Learn, Grow

Keep an open mind that life provides learning opportunities like this every day. Aside from adverse situations, there are people we can learn and grow from. My father provided me a skillset in the market that I was able to leverage during my summer from hell and through the years thereafter. The man I consider my second father, Santo, has been an incredible mentor and role model who I've observed and learned from to grow my consulting business. The same goes for a coaching mentor, Meryl Moritz, who taught me many skills about being an effective coach. She has been a huge influence on my life and career. And lastly, even those tough customers at that retailer taught me valuable lessons, albeit inadvertently. I learned a ton and I evolved because of them.

Flipside of the Coin

On the other side of the coin remains a question unanswered. What could I have learned if I'd handled other adverse situations in my life in a productive manner, such as those times when I may have run from an issue, didn't address a problem, or prematurely quit in the face of too much difficulty? Fortunately, I'm not a quitter, but there are surely times when I could have tested myself further. What lessons and growth did I rob myself of by not putting in full effort or not facing a tough situation head-on? What would have been the result if I had panicked and opted not to help my family when they needed me during the summer from hell? What if I'd run to my safe space? What lessons would I have robbed myself of? Or what if I'd quit Kodak in the midst of the retailer scenario? In both instances, I would have robbed myself of possibly my greatest learnings in facing and growing from adversity. These situations were put in my path to aid me both personally and professionally. My reservoir of options would be barren or limited, that's for sure. For those trials and tribulations, I am forever grateful.

Adversity, problems, and challenges are not going away, so why don't we leverage them to our advantage? While it is painful to lose, struggle, or fail, there is a great upside to learning from these situations, if you are willing to be aware, face it and grow. Every day allots us the opportunity to learn, grow, and develop. Please remember:

"Life is a Classroom; You Are the Student. Class is Always in Session; Always be Grateful!"

A Lesson from a UFC Fighter

I think someone who communicated the perfect perspective on failure after a devastating loss is UFC fighter Eddie Alvarez, who lost in dramatic fashion to UFC champ Conor McGregor. Now, to be sure, McGregor is no slouch, and is possibly the best fighter in UFC history, but Alvarez is pretty darn good. So, losing in such a definitive way was devastating for him. Or was it? After the fight, during an interview, Eddie Alvarez said the following:

"I think there's a freedom in having your worst nightmare come true. As a fighter, your worst nightmare is to get knocked out in front of millions of people. That's like the dream of waking up naked in your classroom. So, getting that out of the way, there's a freedom in it for me. I never thought it would happen. I never pictured it or visualized it ever happening to me, and it happened. I realized after it happened, nothing changed. Nothing changed. My family is still here; my friends are still here. I'm still the same person. Everybody just wants me to fight again and do well again. Nothing really changed. So, there's a freedom in it, and if you haven't experienced it then you won't be able to feel the freedom that I have right now." [31]

What an incredible attitude to have after such a devastating loss. There was a silver lining for Alvarez. In fact, there were several. And, no doubt, that loss will serve him well in the future. And so will yours. Your losses, difficulties, and problems can and will serve you if you let them. If you grow from them, learn from them, and leverage them to your advantage in the future, you will succeed. That is the purpose of this book, and why it is called *In Defense of Adversity*. Adversity has a negative connotation, but it shouldn't. It occurs for our benefit. Accept and acknowledge it.

In closing this point, I think it appropriate to share this incredible quote by Charles Kettering:

"Honestly face defeat; never fake success. Exploit the failure; don't waste it. Learn all you can from it. Never use failure as an excuse for not trying again."

Whether or not he was aware of this quote, Eddie Alvarez lives this belief. He was not defeated. It was an opportunity to learn, an experience to help him grow and become a better MMA practitioner and person for the future. He leveraged a devastating defeat into a sense of gratitude and motivation.

An Attitude of Gratitude

Another way to best handle the trials and tribulations in our lives is to live a life of gratitude. Every day of my life, I pray and meditate on things I'm grateful for. I do this first thing in the morning, several times during the day, and before I go to bed. It keeps me grounded, and it reminds me of how fortunate I am for things, situations, and people— good and bad—that have crossed my path through the years. These situations and people helped mold me into the person I am today, and for that, I'm grateful.

SAGE INSIGHTS

Think of things you're grateful for. If you can't think of anything, I'll give you a few. 95% of you reading this probably have healthy bodies; all your limbs; two working eyes and ears; live in America (a free country); have food on your table; a roof over your head and clothes on your back (can't say the same for some other countries); a vehicle to get places; live in a world with the Internet, which provides the most opportunity to get things done and also make a living more than any other time in the history of the world. If you have a wife and kids who are still with you and love you, this is a great thing, too! Be grateful for what you have! An attitude of gratitude will allow you to solve your problems more effectively and put your life in perspective.

- *Matt Arroyo, Brazilian jiu-jitsu black belt, coach, entrepreneur former UFC athlete*

Helpful Quotes on Gratitude:

- *Gratitude opens the door to … the power, the wisdom, the creativity of the universe. You open the door through gratitude.* —Deepak Chopra

- *The more grateful you are, the more you get to be grateful about. It's that simple.* —Louise Hay

- *Gratitude is the fairest blossom which springs from the soul.* — Henry Ward Beecher

- *Learn to be thankful for what you already have, while you pursue all that you want.* —Jim Rohn

- *Gratitude can transform common days into thanksgiving, turn routine jobs into joy, and change ordinary opportunities into blessings.* —William Arthur Ward

One last quote on gratitude, that also speaks to the crux of this book—through our difficulties lie opportunity and growth:

- *Some people grumble that roses have thorns; I am grateful that thorns have roses.* —Alphonse

Concluding Thoughts—From Coal to Diamonds

What a wonderful quote to end on. It speaks to both the importance of adversity—the thorn in the rose—but also being grateful or optimistic and seeing the rose, not the thorn. It ties into Chad Hymas' point about the lens in which you view adversity as well. This is like the coal to diamonds metaphor. An ugly, dirty piece of black coal can be transformed with years of pressure into a beautiful diamond, just like the immigrant families from my little coal-mining town. Just like me, during my summer from hell, my tough retailer, or the many tricky situations I've faced and overcome. And I'm sure, just like all of you reading this book.

The Epiphany

About four years ago at Christmas, I asked my dad if he wanted to take a drive to Langeloth, the small village within Burgettstown. As we drove through the small village filled with tiny, unattractive tenement houses, he started pointing out where people were raised. *"This was my home, there is Barry Alvarez's home ... and Dr. Maropis, Dr. Spanogians, Dr. Stracci, the Brunner family, the Vallina family, Fernandez family ..."* and on, and on. I knew we had some very successful people come from my hometown, but it hit me like a ton of bricks that day just how successful they were, though many initially came here with little to nothing except determination, love, grit, and a positive attitude. It was at that point that I decided I was going to write this book.

This book started as a labor of love and as an opportunity to pay homage to my hometown. I grew up with so many wonderful, hard-working, morally grounded, loving people. It was a close-knit town as well, filled with many immigrants. We never cared about our backgrounds, although we sometimes teased each other relentlessly about our heritage, yet no one got mad, no one was offended. In our town, immigrant background and desire to succeed in this great country was the common bond. When you played football for the Burgettstown Blue Devils, you didn't care what background your teammates had; we were brothers who fought tooth and nail to succeed and win and we loved each other. It was a wonderful place to be raised, and I wouldn't have wanted it any other way.

In addition, I tied that experience of growing up in Burgettstown with my frustrations today about how so many people complain and moan about America and the opportunity it provides. It's the same country, even if the attitudes may have changed. I don't know, but it was at that time I decided I was going to write a book that at the least had this area as a foundation, or backdrop to build from.

Over the last four years, I've had the great pleasure of interviewing many from Burgettstown, including my father, Barry Alvarez, Dr. Petro Maropis, his with Despina and their boys Chris and Adoni, Pete Stracci, and Brian Petrucci, and their stories greatly inspired me. Their familial journeys were more difficult than I first imagined, yet they were captivating. The common bond was adversity. The trials they faced made them who they were.

Around the same time, I met Coach Eric Parker, who taught me about brain functionality, and then tying in my expertise with the DISC Behavioral Assessment it all came together as a better understanding about my life and situations that made me who I was, both good and bad. It was then that I realized how difficulties were meant for us to succeed, just like those people from my hometown. Adversity made them who they were. It made me who I was. Hence the title and content of this book, *In Defense of Adversity—Turning Your Toughest Challenges Into Your Greatest Success.*

Food for Thought, and Moving Forward

What moments have transformed you? What situations and moments will do so in the future? How will you look at adversity going forward? This book provides both insights and practical tools to leverage adversity to your advantage, and to realize that when troubles manifest, they do so for a reason. This will transform you from a piece of coal to a shining diamond for the entire world to see and experience.

Invictus

Finally, I'll end with a poem by William Ernest Henley called "Invictus." Invictus means "undefeated," invincible," or "unconquerable" in Latin. This poem is the perfect ending to this book. In 2000, Art Berg gave a speech about his favorite poem, "Invictus," to the Baltimore Ravens. Berg, a quadriplegic, was a motivational speaker and wheelchair athlete. The team went on to use the poem as their inspiration, and awarded Mr. Berg a Super Bowl ring after their victory in 2001. [32]

> *Out of the night that covers me,*
> *Black as the pit from pole to pole,*
> *I thank whatever gods may be*
> *For my unconquerable soul.*
>
> *In the fell clutch of circumstance*
> *I have not winced nor cried aloud.*
> *Under the bludgeonings of chance*
> *My head is bloody, but unbowed.*
>
> *Beyond this place of wrath and tears*
> *Looms but the Horror of the shade,*
> *And yet the menace of the years*
> *Finds and shall find me unafraid.*
>
> *It matters not how strait the gate,*
> *How charged with punishments the scroll,*
> *I am the master of my fate,*
> *I am the captain of my soul.*

READER CALL TO ACTION

1. List 3-5 Key Takeaways/Learnings from Chapter 13.

2. List at least 10-20 things you can be grateful for every day.

3. How can you remind yourself daily about these items of gratitude?

CHAPTER 14

SAGE INSIGHTS FROM THE
HIGHLY SUCCESSFUL

He was not born a king of men ... but a child of the common people,
who made himself a great persuader, therefore a leader by dint of firm
resolve, patient effort and dogged perseverance ... he was open to all
impressions and influences and gladly profited by the teachings of
events and circumstances no matter how adverse of unwelcome. There
was probably no year when he was not a wiser, cooler, and better man
than he had been the year preceding.

~

-Horace Greeley-

I end this book with a quote about a man who touched countless lives and still does. Abraham Lincoln, a man who faced many obstacles, overcame them to become one of America's greatest presidents. These words were said about him by one of his greatest adversaries. I end with this quote as I want this book to provide needed insights to help you aspire to be viewed as Lincoln is in this quote. I know it's what I aspire to become. Someone who looks at every day as a chance to learn, grow, gain wisdom, and be a better person with each and every passing day. Every day allots us the opportunity to do it.

In closing, I want to share insights from over 60 people I surveyed, and interviewed who are highly successful. These people did not become successful out of luck. It was through hard work, persistence, perseverance, and of course, facing, overcoming, and learning from the adversity in their lives. They did not become successful without adversity, they became successful in spite of it.

These people come from many different industries, roles, and responsibilities. They are businessmen and women, athletes, both pro and amateur, educators, and are all leaders and influencers in their own right.

I've summarized the top five findings within each of the six questions asked. In addition, I also added seven actual responses for each of these six questions as well. I hope you find these insights as valuable and informative as I did. These people went beyond the call of duty to provide outstanding heartfelt comments for you, the reader. I hope you are as moved as much as I was. I hope they help you in your journey through life as well.

DEVELOPMENTAL TOOLS

To see a comprehensive review of responses by these highly successful individuals, visit www.gavatorta.com. Then click on the *In Defense of Adversity* book icon, and go to the **IDOA Resources** to download all responses by these individuals. See **Sage Insights** area.

Question #1: How do you view adversity, difficulties, and roadblocks when they occur? What is your immediate reaction, and how do you ultimately face these obstacles, moving them out of your way?

- Most viewed adversity as a blessing, a gift, a challenge.

- Most looked at adversity as a temporary setback, nothing permanent.

- Many initially were unhappy about adversity hitting, but quickly transitioned into a resolution mode—what do I need to do now?

- Many viewed adversities as a step toward greater things and goal accomplishment.

- These successful people have learned to leverage adversity to their advantage.

SAGE INSIGHTS

I view adversity, difficulties, and roadblocks as temporary setbacks that are keeping me from where I want to go. Any worthy cause is going to come with a series of difficulties. If you understand that before you begin, it allows you to more easily handle setbacks. My immediate reaction usually varies between anger and disappointment but quickly transitions to "what needs to be done to overcome the problem?" Once the true problem is diagnosed, I put a plan together in order to overcome it. After the plan is in place, I usually find that any concern or anxiety disappears and is replaced with a faith and excitement to overcome.

- Joe Rossi, Defensive Quality Control Coach—University of Minnesota Football

Like everyone, I want to avoid adversity or roadblocks as much as possible. But, I have also learned that as a business owner and working mom, they seem to find me anyway! In my book, *Choose Resilience*, I share my own experiences with adversity and come to the conclusion that I can handle obstacles better when two things are in place: 1) I proactively seek some difficulties so I can address them on my time schedule and 2) when I feel I am at my most creative in order to avoid a bigger problem later.

- Jen Shirkani, Author, EGO VS EQ and Choose Resilience

Adversity is a gift as it challenges me to put all that I have learned to work, finding solutions, executing those solutions and eventually celebrating the success when I overcome the adverse situation. My immediate reaction to adversity is to stop, breathe, think, and then formulate a plan of attack. The best way to move adverse situations out of my way is to take them on, head- on, enlisting the assistance of others when appropriate.

- Adam Gross, Sr. Director of Sales—Dippin' Dots LLC.

I love a challenge. And with all challenges, there are unexpected setbacks. This is also part of the process. As challenges, I love new problems. Each problem is met with a can-do attitude. My initial thoughts are how to deal with the problem, not why something cannot be done. In fact, dwelling on all the potential issues instead of solutions actually upsets me when I see others pointing out all the reasons something cannot be done.

- Ron Bonnstetter, Sr. Vice President of Research & Development at Target Training International

I never view an adversity as permanent. I have a confidence that things will always work out. If it is something that I can control, I believe that I will work my way through it. My son once asked me what I would do if I was homeless and I answered that I would never be homeless. He was after what I would do if I had no place to go and I just could not see myself in that situation.

- *Ed Pinkham, Defensive Coordinator—University of Massachusetts Football*

My reaction has depended on my level of self-confidence at the time of the occurrence. In the times of my highest self-confidence, I immediately formulate a plan to overcome the obstacle and set ideal, realistic, and acceptable timelines and outcomes for overcoming the roadblock. In moments of weakness, I have known myself to lost clarity of my ultimate goal and become depressed about the onset of unexpected adversity. Once I have regained perspective on the long-term goal or stepped back away temporarily from the situation, a detailed plan is usually executed with determination.

-*Brian Hill, National Sales Executive at Modern Enterprise Solutions*

I view adversity as an opportunity. Adversity is never welcomed but when it arises, it presents an opportunity to grow as a person or professional, despite the outcome. Depending on the situation, my reaction may vary. Ultimately, in order to overcome any adversity, I assess the situation and break down the steps I think are necessary to overcome it.

-Keeno Griffin, Account Executive, former wrestling National Champion, Newberry College

Question #2: *How do you learn from the adversity you face in your life? How has adversity been helpful to you?*

- The realization that adversity is temporary.

- The more difficulties faced and overcome, the stronger for the future.

- Adversity shaped these people into who they were meant to become.

- The difficult times were seen as an opportunity to reflect, not react.

- Adversity made these people who they were meant to be.

SAGE INSIGHTS

Must view adversity as learning opportunities. Difficulties exist for a reason, otherwise we would be omnipotent beings. I also view them as revealing. It forces us to view things from a different perspective, which leads to growth and understanding.

- Brady Quinn, CFB/NFL Analyst Fox Sports and former QB, Notre Dame and National Football League (NFL)

Without adversity, I would not be the person I am today, so I am grateful for those difficult times in my life. Throughout my life I was faced with adversity such as single parenthood, financial struggles, divorce, work stress, health issues and loss of a job. Now I often have to remind myself that adversity is part of life. Accepting adversity helps you overcome it. The difficult times in life help us appreciate when things are going smoothly.

- Margie Bahm, Sales Manager, Fortune 500 Company

I believe you learn from every experience, good or bad. That's what life is about, learning and growing. When faced with a challenge, I may not be focused on what I will take away from it, but I like to reflect on my experiences and understand how they've helped me to grow. Reflecting on the adversity I've seen in my life helps me to address situations differently and with new focus.

- Sarah Peeples, Training Manager at Stanley Black & Decker

Adversity causes pain and we learn from pain. Without pain, we would never grow or change or prosper. Life is boring without adversity and pain. Facing adversity and pain head-on is a blessing. We might not overcome the adversity right away, but it's a God-given adversity and the longer it takes to resolve, the greater the value to the individual.

- Topher Cramm, Senior National Account Manager at Stanley Convergent Security

The more adversity I have faced, the more I have learned to persevere and when disappointment happens, something great, often better, is right around the corner.

- David Sedmak, Head Football Coach, Desert Mountain High School

Learning from adversity is critical to long-term success. Every day is filled with roadblocks and difficulties. Using your experiences from adversity will drive successful results. Human nature is filled with adversity and giving up isn't an option. I look at adversity as an opportunity to change the game and come back with solutions to problems for our customers and team.

- Dave Pruitt, Vice President of National Accounts and Training at Stanley

Convergent Security

Adversity has been a constant companion, in inspiring ways and in dark ones. I believe deeply that we can learn from a happy place as much as a challenging one. But there is no denying that when we are under pressure we are forced to grow. I learned from my depression that I am not defined by the thoughts in my head. I learned that my brain and my soul are two separate things and that my brain has the ability to mislead me. I have learned from the adversity I've experienced in business that you have to trust your gut; it rarely lies. I've learned from adversity in relationships that there is a delicate balance between loving yourself and loving others, and that selfish isn't always a bad word.

- *Roni Sloman, Certified Life Coach and founder, owner of Bella Prana Yoga Studio*

Question #3: How have you leveraged adversity to your advantage? What have you gained or learned that you wouldn't have if you'd given up?

- Developed patience ... the realization that it was time to step back to think and plan.

- Many viewed adversity as a challenge to be overcome, not overtaken.

- Viewed as a chance to grow, and the experience of it— accepting it as a part of life and growth.

- Pushed beyond previous limitations, and stretched further than originally thought.

- A good attitude is key to addressing and overcoming. Not panicking, seeing options.

SAGE INSIGHTS

Adversity taught me to develop resilience, and resilience was my part of my arsenal of success. The advantage was being persistent and never giving up when times were difficult. I've learned that roadblocks are endless and at times, challenging. By developing resilience, the roadblocks are easier to deal with, especially at times when everything is falling apart. I have learned if I had avoided adversity and not addressed it for what it was, failure was inevitable.

- Mark Marshall, Sales Executive, college wrestling coach, adjunct professor at Seton Hill University

Adversity has built my strength and confidence but also helped me be humble which are traits I use every day, all day long. If I'd given up, I would never have realized my potential and all I am capable of.

- Karen Lindsey, Executive Coach & Leadership Development Consultant at Lindsey Resources

I believe adversity has provided me with motivation even in times when I was not successful and had to deal with a transition in career or in my life. It's forced me to not forget, but to carry it with me as motivation to provide that drive in moments of difficulty that lie ahead, potentially providing guidance, depending on what that difficulty is.

- Billy Quarantillo, Professional MMA Fighter, contestant on Season 22 of The Ultimate Fighter

Adversity brings out creativity and meaning in the work that I do. During challenging situations where solutions do not seem feasible is when I am best able to craft new ideas and find a solution. Adversity also makes me questions what I value, and in turn I discover what motivates me and what my true values are.

- Karina T, Market Manager at Fortune 500 Company

Overcoming something, anything, is the greatest feeling ever and makes you grow in confidence, in spirit, in life. You learn that if you simply hang on and keep climbing ... that eventually you will get somewhere. You will find the way, the pinnacle of what it is you're are going after. The simple lesson is that if you simply don't give up ... something will happen positively. A few sayings come to mind: God helps those who help themselves. Fatigue makes cowards of us all. The latter is from Vince Lombardi.

- Adoni Maropis, Actor/Athlete/Type 1 Diabetic

The feeling once the adversity is overcome can be intoxicating. In my opinion the more strenuous and stressful while going through it, the more rewarding the experience once resolved. It has molded me into what I am today and what I will be in the future. I believe there are two different types of stress: eustress and distress. Eustress is productive and growth oriented while distress can be destructive in nature. I try to view everything as eustress and not let it become distressful.

- Robert Tudi, GM Tudi Mechanical Systems

I've used adversity to grow and appreciate the people in my life. I pay attention to life and my surroundings more after difficult situation occurs. It has allowed me to be less self-focused and care more about others, especially given that it is usually those close to you that help you through tough times. I believe everything happens for a reason, even if it is painful, but in the end things are set in motion for you to be the best person you were meant to be.

- Lisa Sideris, Sr. Account Executive at a Big Four Accounting Firm

Question #4: *How do you remain positive during times of adversity? What self-talk, affirmations, or sources of inspiration do you call on to keep you motivated and moving during tough times?*

- Deeply personal—what works for one doesn't for another … it runs the gamut … you need to find out what does and doesn't work for you.

- Staying positive during adversity was a key common-thread factor.

- Many relied on spiritual faith—a belief in a higher power, prayer.

- Simply put … the opportunity to practice resilience.

- The realization that a lesson, or lessons will be learned— strengthening for the future.

SAGE INSIGHTS

Prayer. Faith in God. Self-reflection. Learning. Being around those I love and trust. Unwavering belief in myself. Staying humble. No sense of entitlement. Adversity has resulted in me truly finding my true, authentic self and stay consistently authentic. And always determined to make God and my family proud.

- Pam Sedmak, Business Executive at Fortune 500 Company

BREATHE, take a walk, think through it, talk through it. Draw on those past experiences and never give up. Persistence many times is the key. Take a different look, approach from a different perspective. Perspective is also key. By talking it through internally and with someone else, perspective can be gained and I find sometimes I will change my entire attitude and approach to a situation and the motivation that comes from that is refreshing at times. Especially when the outcome is successful!

- Holly Blake, West Division Sales Manager at Dippin' Dots

I do a lot of self-talk to stay positive in tough times. I have been a long-time proponent of Neurolinguistic Programming, which is how a person talks to themselves translates into their actions. I stay motivated by looking around the world and thinking that, no matter how tough a position I may be in, or whatever adversity I'm facing, there are people out there who don't have the opportunities I do, so don't squander them or cry during the tough times. What I'm facing pales in comparison to what many other people are living through.

- Kevin Palermo, Financial Consultant at Fortune 500 Company

I am a big 'get away from it' proponent. Give yourself sometime away to enjoy a hobby or time with family and friends. That downtime or time away from the adversity helps you refuel emotionally, giving you the energy and the desire needed to get back to attacking the adversity head-on. I enjoy the mantra of 'control what you can control' and when you are able to do that the motivation plays a big role to keep attacking things within your control and see little victories along the way to the big outcome.

- Brian Tucker, Head Wrestling Coach at Seton Hill University

It is tough, no doubt. Surrounding yourself with positive, loving people helps. Self-belief, looking back at all you have accomplished and know that setbacks get you ready for big comebacks. Knowing that at the end of the day you will be okay and loved by your friends and family helps.

- Matt Frevola, UFC Athlete & UFC Contender Series Main Card Winner

Without a doubt, it's my faith. Above all that's been number one, but along with that has been my wife who is always there as a champion. After both of those comes my high-achieving peers I connect with on a regular basis. The expression "you become most like those you associate with the most" is so true.

- Mark Hunter CSP, The Sales Hunter and author of High Profit Selling, and High Profit Prospecting

No self-talk or affirmations. Being strong-willed and realizing that there will always be adversity. Looking back on really tough times in my life and knowing that I have broken through to create positive outcomes is my drive.

-Todd Fox, Director of Distribution at Target Training International

Question #5: *What habits, hobbies, or rituals do you practice that help you face adversity in a good frame of mind?*

- Deeply personal—what works for one doesn't for another ... it runs the gamut ... you need to find out what does and doesn't work for you.

- Nearly all had some form of exercise or approach to focus on health—physically, mentally, spiritually, and emotionally.

- Spiritual reflection—getting away. Prayer, music, and meditation were common themes.

- Most all reflected on gratitude—things they were truly grateful in their lives.

- Heavy reliance on family, friends, and loved ones to carry them through the difficult times.

SAGE INSIGHTS

Yoga, Pilates, church/prayer. I try and put myself in adverse situations in my brain beforehand so when those adverse situations happen it's like I've already been there. I try and train so hard so that anything that happens to me is not as hard as my training.

-Keith Tandy, Defensive Back with the Tampa Bay Buccaneers

I think taking a step back and leaving the situation for a moment can help clear my mind and help refocus the energy needed to succeed. Spending time with my family centers me and allows me to be a better employee on Monday morning.

- Rob Newman, Director Business Development at Stanley Black & Decker

Reference points from the past ... as early as my college years, I remember sitting for an important exam (that would grant me distinction in my major or not) fretting that I would never finish in the allotted time. I suddenly recalled that I was as fearful about my second attempt to pass my driver's test and I did so with flying colors. Looking back for evidence of having gotten through tough times helps me have faith in myself and faith overall in a higher intelligence that this, too, shall pass!

- Meryl Moritz, Master Certified Coach at Meryl Moritz Resources

Exercise. Get outside in nature. It helps me re-frame my mind and realize the bigger picture. I constantly have a book that is not work related that I am reading. This allows for me to have my alone time without the mind racing with what-ifs.

- Sarah Sponaugle, D.C., Chiropractic Practitioner at Driven Health & Fitness

For me, I start each day with reflection and prayer. I go to my sources of strength. For me, the reflections are geared toward what I have in my life. My blessings, and also my reason to keep moving forwards. I rely on daily prayer for strength, inspiration and provision. Whatever your faith or beliefs, go to that source for daily renewal. I also find that daily physical exercise provides a greater sense of confidence and greater reserves of energy and focus.

- Mark Liebel, Chief Operating Officer at Dippin' Dots

I have learned to take a beat, stop what I am doing, and pull back and just wait. I have also been known to start an email to no one and write an emotional or reactive response that I pretend I am sending to that person or persons. Then I read it (sometimes several times) and do a gut check to see if the way I am reacting and sounding is who I want to be. I also decide, is this my hill today? Is this worth using my energy? Most of the time, I delete it and feel a peace that allows me to let it go. Being in my 40s has also allowed me the time to understand what Robin Roberts of GMA says, 'everyone's got something' and I may not be aware of their something and that may be playing a big part in the way they are acting, treating me, or behaving. So if I choose to give them power, then I need to find the strength to fight back, otherwise I think about what I have, who I love, and that always trumps any asshole any day of the week!

- Kim Milite, Eastern Division Manager at Dippin' Dots

Physical exercise has always been a stress reducer for me. It is also very important not to react too quickly when faced with an adverse situation. Analyzing and looking at all options/risks that will give you the outcome you want.

-Pete Comis, Head of National Accounts at Bayer ES

Question #6: *Who are the people that you look up to? Why do they stand out in your mind?*

- Deeply personal—what works for one doesn't for another ... it runs the gamut ... you need to find out what does and doesn't work for you.

- Family members—especially parents and grandparents.

- Other highly successful people in their lives and/or role models to aspire to (coaches—athletic, personal/professional, historical figures, athletes).

- Many chose common people who became successful in their own rights, despite great odds.

- Spiritual, biblical, higher power inspirational characters.

SAGE INSIGHTS

I like reading books on other leaders to see how they handled their careers, but not books on business leaders—more political leaders. One book I read fairly recently was the biography of Harry Truman (written by the historian David McCullough). It demonstrated Truman's tenacity, toughness, yet humbleness of handling some very difficult decisions, so I look up to him. I also look up to anyone who has persevered, no matter how tough the odds are. Another good example of this is the Wright Brothers ... they had many reasons and opportunities to quit learning how to accomplish powered flight, but they simply would not give up.

- Michael Barrette, Chief Marketing & Sales Officer at Dippin' Dots & Doc Popcorn

I admire people without egos, self-effacing, successful, and always positive. I admire people that have accomplished a lot and enjoy reading or watching or hearing as to how they have done it.

- Peter Vaas, Former Pro & College Football coach, owner of Everything Football, LLC

I look up to the people who are successful in life. I believe everyone has a certain genius. The people who I admire most are the ones who develop that genius to its maximum capacity. I have a friend who could remember the snap count from the huddle to the line of scrimmage and he was the center. He wasn't book-smart but he now is a mechanic for American Airlines. His genius is he could fix anything. That, I admire

- Robert Fraser, Assistant Football Coach, Ohio State

Kevin Harrington is definitely a mentor of mine. He is a phenomenal man. He is uber successful, but yet kind and generous to everyone. He gave me an opportunity when I was no one and I had just started my company. I try now to do the same for others who are just starting out, to help them either by giving advice, attending their events, or just being an ear to listen.

- Tara Richter, Owner of Richter Publishing

I look up to my parents and my two older brothers the most. I never had to venture beyond our dinner table to find my heroes because they were all assembled there. The one who I always looked up to the most was my older brother Adoni, who was diagnosed with Type I diabetes when he was 18 months old. He always had to endure so much more than the rest of us. Having diabetes is such a burden, but thanks to his winner's mindset, he has done very well. I look up to all of them because they are exemplary and exceptional people. They are amazing role models. I've been very blessed.

- Chris Maropis, Sports Medicine Physician

Where I work we often come in contact with Paralympians. It always amazes me that these athletes do more with less and you never see them complain. These types of people inspire me more than anyone else.
One thing I've learned ... Adversity teaches us to have greater compassion for others in their hours of adversity. Everyone is fighting a battle we know nothing about.

-John Mahoney, Basketball Coach at IMG Academy

My grandfather, my father, my Uncle Roger, my cousin Victor—they have always chased opportunity no matter what their situation was. From early childhood I have never heard them make an excuse or complain about their position in life. As role models they have always offered solutions and always promoted searching for more than what stands right in front of you.

- Luis Echeverry, certified personal trainer, owner of Driven Health & Fitness

READER CALL TO ACTION

1. List 3-5 Key Takeaways/Learnings from the Closing Chapter.

2. Who out of these successful individuals from the Closing Chapter inspired you? Why? Will you follow any of their recommendations? If so, list which ones.

3. List 5-10 steps you'll take after reading this book.

ABOUT THE AUTHOR

Owner of Steve Gavatorta Group, Inc., Steve has coached, trained, and developed thousands of high-performance individuals and teams. He works with many Fortune 500 companies in various industries, which include pharmaceutical/medical equipment, healthcare/hospitals, consumer packaged goods, finance, media/advertising, and small business/retail/franchise businesses.

A consultant, coach, and public speaker, Steve empowers his clients to identify, develop, and exceed their performance goals.

Steve is a Certified Professional Behavioral and Values Analyst (CPBA & CPVA), a certified Myers-Briggs practitioner, and is accredited to coach and train for Emotional Intelligence (EQ).

Steve enjoys martial arts and is a Muay Thai Brazilian jiu-jitsu and yoga practitioner and traveler. He currently resides in Tampa, Florida.

Following Steve Gavatorta:

- Free motivational quotes:
- http://www.gavatorta.com/quote.htm
- Free motivational cards:
- http://www.gavatorta.com/cards.htm
- Facebook: https://www.facebook.com/steve.gavatorta
- Linked In: https://www.linkedin.com/in/gavatorta/
- Twitter: https://twitter.com/SteveGavatorta
- Instagram: https://www.instagram.com/steve_gavatorta/

CITED REFEENCES

CHAPTER 1: Ad Astra Per Aspera ...Through Hardships to the Stars

1. DeArdo, B. (2016, March 2). *WATCH James Harrisons appearance on the Steve Harvey Show*. Retrieved from http://247sports.com

2. Biography.com Editors. (2016, November 16). *Steve Harvey Biography*. Retrieved from https://www.biography.com

3. Carrejo, C. (2016, June 28). *These Inspiring Pat Summitt Quotes Will Motivate You to Work Harder Every Day*. Retrieved from https://www.bustle.com

4. Mielach, D. (2014, March 19). *10 Inspirational Quotes from Today's Top Entrepreneurs*. Retrieved from http://www.businessnewsdaily.com

5. Melnik, P. (2014, March 12). *Adversity gives garnacha grape its qualities*. Retrieved from http://www.pressdemocrat.com

6. Cramm, Shelley S., General Editor, *NIV God's Word for Gardeners Bible* (Grand Rapids, Mich., Zondervan, 2014), pages 1215-1220.

7. Favale, D. (2013, February 14). *Michael Jordan's Unofficial Guide to Success In the NBD*. Retrieved from http://bleacherreport.com

8. Woodall, T. (2015, September 8). *Michael Jordan – Obstacles Don't have to stop you. If you run into a wall*. Retrieved from http://www.goalgettingpodcast.com

9. Rowling, J.K. (2008, June 5). *Text of J.K. Rowling's speech*. Retrieved from https://www.news.harvard.edu

10. Washington, D. (2011, May). *Denzel Washington - Graduation Speech*. Retrieved from http://blackeconomics.co.uk

11. Gardner, S. (2017, January 9). *Rocky Bleier recalls Vietnam War, 40 years after it ended*. Retrieved from http://www.foxsports.com

12. Forbes.com Editors. (2017). *America's Richest Self-Made Women*. Retrieved from https://www.forbes.com

13. Maxfield, J. (2014, February 10). *Here's Why Bill Gates Was So Much Richer Thank Steve Jobs*. https://www.fool.com

14. Nafte, D. (2017*). The Journey of Walt Disney*. Retrieved from

http://www.successstorysunday.com

CHAPTER 3: Building a Foundation and Environment To Grind

15. Gonzalez, G. (2017, September 27). *Tony Robbins reveals 3 tips that made him a megamillionire.* Retrieved from https://www.cnbc.com

CHAPTER 5: High D, Dominant Style

* With the exception of personal stories and clarifying points, most of the content in this chapter describing attributes of the Dominant Style was taken from the following source:

16. Bonnstetter, Bill J., and Judy I. Suiter. (2016). *The Universal Language DISC: A Reference Manual.* (pp. 57-67). Arizona. Target Training International, Ltd.

CHAPTER 6: HIGH I, Influencer Style

* With the exception of personal stories and clarifying points, most of the content in this chapter describing attributes of the Influencer Style was taken from the following source:

17. Bonnstetter, Bill J., and Judy I. Suiter. (2016). *The Universal Language DISC: A Reference Manual.* (pp. 73-85). Arizona. Target Training International, Ltd.

CHAPTER 7: High S, Steadiness Style

* With the exception of personal stories and clarifying points, most of the content in this chapter describing attributes of the Steadiness Style was taken from the following source:

18. Bonnstetter, Bill J., and Judy I. Suiter. (2016). *The Universal Language DISC: A Reference Manual.* (pp. 91-101). Arizona. Target Training International, Ltd.

CHAPTER 8: High C, Compliant Style

* With the exception of personal stories and clarifying points, most of the content in this chapter describing attributes of the Compliant Style was taken from the following source:

19. Bonnstetter, Bill J., and Judy I. Suiter. (2016). *The Universal Language DISC: A Reference Manual.* (pp. 107-117). Arizona. Target Training International, Ltd.

CHAPTER 9: Emotional Triggers & Responses

20. Franzi, R. (2016, January 7). *What I learned this week from Jen Shirkani, Author of EGO vs EQ.* Retrieved from http://www.criticalmassforbusiness.com

21. Goleman, G. (2004, January). *What Makes a Leader?* Retrieved from https://hbr.org

22. Bonnstetter, Bill J., and Judy I. Suiter. (2016). *The Universal Language DISC: A Reference Manual.* (pp. 59). Arizona. Target Training International, Ltd.

23. Bonnstetter, Bill J., and Judy I. Suiter. (2016). *The Universal Language DISC: A Reference Manual.* (pp. 76). Arizona. Target Training International, Ltd.

24. Bonnstetter, Bill J., and Judy I. Suiter. (2016). *The Universal Language DISC: A Reference Manual.* (pp. 93). Arizona. Target Training International, Ltd.

25. Bonnstetter, Bill J., and Judy I. Suiter. (2016). *The Universal Language DISC: A Reference Manual.* (pp. 109). Arizona. Target Training International, Ltd.

CHAPTER 10: Successfully Interacting with Others

26. Lombardi, Vince, Jr. (2001). *What it Takes to be #1.* (pp. 208). New York. McGraw Hill

27. Alvarez, Barry., and Mike Lucas. (2006). *Don't Flinch. Barry Alvarez: Autobiography.* (pp. 77). Illinois. KCI Sports, LLC.

* With the exception of personal stories and clarifying points, much of the content in this chapter describing cues for effective communication and interaction with the 4 DISC Styles was taken from the following source:

28. Bonnstetter, Bill J., and Judy I. Suiter. (2016). *The Universal Language DISC: A Reference Manual.* (pp. 68-119). Arizona. Target Training International, Ltd.

CHAPTER 12: Strengthening the Foundation

29. Covey, S. (2017). *The 7 Habits of Highly Effective People: Habit 7 - Sharpen the Saw.* Retrieved from https://www.stephencovey.com

30. Widrich, L. (2014, February 4). *What Happens to Our Brains When We Exercise and How it Makes Us Happier.* Retrieved from https://www.fastcompany.com

CHAPTER 13: Life's Class is Always in Session; Always be Attentive and Grateful

31. Meshew, J. (2017, May 9). *Eddie Alvarez on Conor McGregor loss: There's a freedom in having your worst nightmare come true.* Retrieved from https://www.mmafighting.com

32. Desert News Editors. (2002, February 22). *Motivational speaker Art E. Berg dies at 39.* Retrieved from http://www.deseretnews.com

Made in the USA
Las Vegas, NV
19 August 2021

28450654R00105